Classroom Organization and Management

Grades 3–5

Strategies for Establishing and Maintaining an Effective Learning Environment

Lisa Dellamora
SENIOR AUTHOR

Sarah Csernica Llanes
CO-AUTHOR

Illustrated by Becky Radtke

To Sarah Csernica Llanes I can't believe that it took a trip to Africa to find a friend like you living just across the River! Our strengths balance each other's weaknesses well, and our decorating skills are both sheer talent and a brilliant distraction to our writing efforts! You are the definition of a true friend don't ever forget that or let anyone tell you otherwise. Thanks for sharing her with me, John! xoxo, Lisa

To Elaine Chugranis How could I not include you here? I miss our regular subway debriefing rides already! You have been a friend who has helped me to see and think about things that I see and do every day in very different ways. Thanks for pointing out when I was wrong, and for helping me to see when I was right. I've learned a lot from you, friend. Power!!! Beauty!!! xoxo, Lisa

And, finally, and most importantly,
To my mother and father, who have always been there for me, even during the times when I may not have been. You may not hear me say it enough, but know that I love you both dearly. Thank you for being who you are, and for helping me to become who I am. I love you, Lisa

To my beautiful mother Thank you for being my first teacher.
For my dad and my brother, for Rebecca and Valerie Thanks for loving me unconditionally.
To my hubby Thanks for pushing me to challenge myself every day. I love you! Sarah

Deepest appreciation for their submissions: Lisa Bernstein, Mary Clancy, Amy Goodman, and Beth McDonald

Rigby • Saxon • Steck-Vaughn

ISBN: 0-7398-9951-1
© 2006 Harcourt Achieve Inc.

All rights reserved. Harcourt Achieve Inc. grants permission to duplicate enough copies of the reproducible pages to distribute to students. Other than these specifically allowed pages, no part of the material protected by this copyright may be reproduced or utilized in any form or by any means, in whole or in part, without permission in writing from the copyright owner. Requests for permission should be mailed to: Copyright Permissions, Harcourt Achieve Inc., P.O. Box 27010, Austin, Texas 78755.

Rigby and Steck-Vaughn are trademarks of Harcourt Achieve Inc. registered in the United States of America and/or other jurisdictions.

Printed in the United States of America.

1 2 3 4 5 6 7 8 9 862 09 08 07 06 05

Contents

Preface 4
Introduction 8
    General Beliefs About Intermediate Students ... 8
    Building a Solid Foundation 10
    Effective Instruction Begins with Classroom Management 12
    Section Overviews 22

Section 1: Creating a Climate Conducive to Learning 23

Chapter 1: Organizing for Space 24
    How Does the Classroom Feel? 26
    How Does the Classroom Look? 30
    How Does the Classroom Sound? 44

Chapter 2: Organizing for Time 46
    Finding Time to Fit It All In 46
    Scheduling: Putting the Puzzle Pieces Together .. 48
    Creating More Minutes in the Day 50

Chapter 3: Organizing for Assessment 63
    Informal Assessment 64
    Formal Assessment 69
    Finding the Time 75
    Keeping Track of It All 76
    Sharing It All with Others 77

Section 2: Setting the Tone for the Rest of the Year 79

Chapter 4: Establishing Ongoing Routines 80
    Rules vs. Expectations 80
    Organizing and Managing Your Classroom for Optimal Effectiveness: Ongoing Routines 83

Chapter 5: Putting It All Together for the First Weeks of School 96
    Before School Starts 96
    The First Day of School 97
    The First Week of School 99
    Week Two 102
    Week Three 104
    Week Four and Beyond 106
    Handling Challenging Behavior 107

Section 3: Managing Independent Work Time 113

Chapter 6: Management Systems 114
    Teacher-Led Management Systems 116
    Student-Directed Management Systems 119

Chapter 7: Organizing Stations with Engaging Activities 121
    Classroom Library 122
    Poetry Station 125
    Writing Station 126
    Penmanship Station 130
    Art Station 131
    Word Zone 133
    Listening Station 136

Appendix 138
Bibliography 159

Preface

The way a teacher handles a difficult situation with an intermediate student can determine the student's immediate reaction, as well as set the foundation for all future interactions with that student, and possibly other students, in the classroom. As experienced teachers across the intermediate grades, we share the firm belief that the teacher sets the tone that determines the eventual outcome of nearly all situations in the classroom, and, ultimately, the degree of success or failure of teaching and learning that will occur that year.

Intermediate students are maturing and developing physically and cognitively in ways that may often result in our forgetting that they are still young children and are in need of strong leadership and support so that they can function successfully within the classroom. It is our belief that the teacher is the keystone that holds everything together in a classroom. Each year will differ, but a "good year" cannot be attributed to a "good class." A "good year" is attributable to a "good teacher," one who is a masterful educator, an effective organizer, and a manager who is successful at developing self-managing skills and behaviors within the students in that classroom.

As we were planning for this book, sharing stories of effective and not-so-effective classroom management practices from our past, we found a striking similarity that underpinned our collective experiences. In every situation we shared about interactions between ourselves and our students, learning occurred both within the students and within ourselves. Every interaction with a student was evaluated in our minds, either formally or informally, and each event worked to strengthen our abilities to handle future situations with exponentially greater finesse. Of course, we had setbacks, bad days, and less than optimal interactions every now and then, but what stands strong throughout all of the stories we shared with one another is that we learned from every one of them. Our students learned too.

Here is a story that Sarah shared that reminded us both of how important it is for a teacher to carefully measure her reactions and responses to student behavior:

The day of the annual science fair came right on time. Unfortunately, Jamal and his science project came a little late—and a little broken. I was busy taking care of the attendance and lunch count (something I later determined could be easily handled by my students, freeing up more of my time!) and, therefore, was not immediately available to him. Jamal began to repeatedly interrupt the morning routine, insisting that I help him fix a part of his project that had broken.

"Miss Csernica! Miss Csernica! Hey! Look! You need to fix this! Look! It's broke! I need you to fix this! HEY!"

"Jamal," I responded in my gentle, but firm 'I must re-establish order' voice, "I'm taking attendance now. This will have to wait. I'll help you when I'm finished."

In typical "beginning of the year" Jamal fashion, his reactive response was to hurl his project to the floor and begin yelling. "I HATE THIS! This is a stupid project! I hate it and I hate you!"

As he kicked his way through the remains of his science project and stormed across the room, I had a moment to reflect. What went through my head was something to the effect of: "No matter

Preface

how frustrated or angry I am at Jamal's behavior, I am the adult in this classroom and I have the responsibility to respond as such." What I needed was a proactive response to Jamal's reactive behavior.

As the leader in this classroom, I had many choices at this point. I could have:

A. taken it personally and reacted angrily, yelling right back at him. "You hate me? Don't you EVER say that! You better get yourself into your seat right now, mister! ... And wipe that look off your face!" (Note: A response like this in an effort to demonstrate "who's in charge here" is sure to continue to elevate the situation to even higher degrees of intensity and frustration.)

B. quickly gone over to him, apologizing, asking if he was okay, and helping him put his project together. "Oh Jamal, I'm SO sorry. Everything will be okay. Don't get angry. Here, I'll pick it up for you. I'll fix it." (Note: A response such as this one would temporarily diffuse the situation, but would not teach Jamal how to handle similar situations in the future. It would also develop a reliance on the teacher to solve problems.)

C. calmly walked to the intercom button, buzzed the office, and then rolled my eyes to the class as I announced, "I'm having another ISSUE with Jamal. Can you please send someone to remove him from the classroom?" (Note: A response of this nature would result in public humiliation in front of his classmates and/or an increase in problematic behavior on Jamal's part.)

D. addressed the situation from the angle of the science project. "And that science project of yours that's on the floor in pieces? That's a big ZERO in my grade book now!" (Note: This response, in the form of a threat, is a diverted effort to re-establish who has the power in this classroom. In this case, Jamal is sure to find some other way to demonstrate his power in the classroom.)

E. ignored the behavior, assuming that it will go away, and the problem would be resolved. (Note: Ignoring people or their behavior doesn't help in addressing the underlying issues at hand. The same is true in a classroom. Jamal's tactic would have been to make it impossible for him to be ignored—the TAP-TAP-TAP with the pen on the desk routine was one of his favorites. Problems cannot be expected to resolve themselves.)

F. calmly addressed Jamal and the situation directly by saying, "Jamal, this is something important that we need to talk about. I will be finished taking the attendance in one minute. After that, everyone will start their independent reading and you and I can talk—either in here or in the hallway, whichever one you choose. Think about where you'd like to talk, and I will be there in one minute, okay?" (Note: This option would allow the tension of the situation to be diffused, but the situation would not be ignored or responded to in a reactive manner, which would have led to greater problems.)

Fortunately for both of us, I chose Option F, and that made all the difference in the world. Giving Jamal the privilege of a calm and rational immediate response and a minute to cool down provided both of us the opportunity to have a healthy and productive conversation. In talking with Jamal, I learned that Jamal's family had been evicted from their apartment the night before and he had spent the night in the family's car with his mother. And his science project.

Preface

Choosing Options A–E could have led to serious, but unintended negative consequences that would have impacted our relationship and the dynamic of the classroom, not only on that day, but on every day thereafter. Choosing to assert my authority in a way that undermined Jamal's character in any way would have been damaging and humiliating to him, and the outcome would not have been a productive one for either of us.

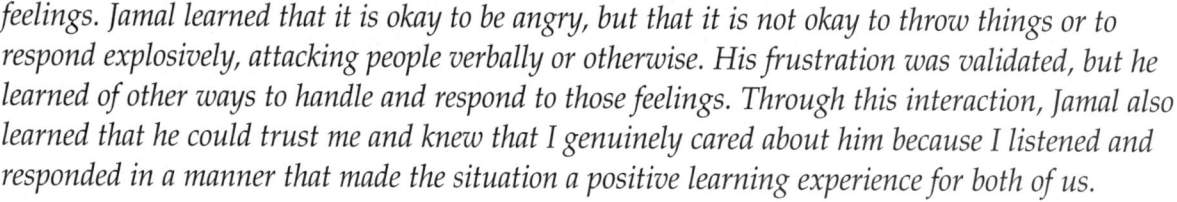

Through the response I chose, I was able to learn some background information on Jamal that was critical to my understanding of Jamal as a person and as a student in my classroom who was up against some powerful odds. I was also able to help Jamal understand that feelings of anger and frustration happen, but that there are productive ways of handling and communicating those feelings. Jamal learned that it is okay to be angry, but that it is not okay to throw things or to respond explosively, attacking people verbally or otherwise. His frustration was validated, but he learned of other ways to handle and respond to those feelings. Through this interaction, Jamal also learned that he could trust me and knew that I genuinely cared about him because I listened and responded in a manner that made the situation a positive learning experience for both of us.

The story of Jamal reminds us that there are innumerable and significant choices to be made as teachers. Jamal reminds us of the importance of being *proactive* as teachers. From the above response options, choices A through E are strongly *reactive* in nature.

Steven Covey, author of the bestseller *The 7 Habits of Highly Effective People*, also teaches us how to be proactive. Covey (1989) describes proactivity as being "more than merely taking initiative. It means that as human beings, we are responsible for our own lives. Our behavior is a function of our decisions, not our conditions"… (71).

A similar message echoes through the scene from the movie *Dangerous Minds* (1995) when Michelle Pfeiffer repeatedly reminds her students "You have a choice!" They respond with an eternity of "but …"; however, she remains steadfast in insisting that no matter what the situation, there is some choice to be made. Whether the choice is in how you react to something or in how you let it affect you, you have a choice. You always have a choice.

Covey (1989) suggests that what you say and how you say it indicates the degree to which you are being proactive. In an academic setting, you can reflect on your words to self-evaluate your level of proactivity as an instructional leader.

The problem with reactive language is that it can become a self-fulfilling prophecy (Covey 1989). Think how long Sarah's school year would have been if she had chosen to respond to Jamal reactively. If he had not helped her realize the importance of being proactive, she most certainly would have failed him that year as a teacher.

Preface

Reactive Language	Proactive Language
• I always get the "bad" students. • That wouldn't work in *my* class. • I have too many students in my class. • He drives the other students crazy. • She drives me crazy. • The principal/fire marshal/district won't let me… • I have to… • I can't… • If only…	• Let's see what I can do. • I'll try it. • I can try a different approach. • I can help the other students learn how to respond. • I will choose an appropriate response. • I can control my own feelings. • I prefer… • I will… • I choose…

Adapted from *The 7 Habits of Highly Effective People* by Steven Covey © 1989 Simon and Schuster.

To hold, daily, in our hands the responsibility of affecting children in powerful and lasting ways is one of the greatest honors we ever have or will be privileged to receive. Education is a profession that brings a complex set of opportunities, challenges, and, ultimately, rewards to both the teacher and the learners. Teaching is an awesome task, to say the least.

This book is an offering to you of our vast research and collective experiences. The best practices for organizing and managing the classroom come from years of working with students in our own classrooms as well as students in others' classrooms, and through leading countless teacher in-services across the country. As you read through this book, pick and choose the strategies that work best for you and your students as you create your own classroom management plan.

> ### Efficiency and Effectiveness Task
>
> **Sorting Proactive and Reactive Statements**
>
> Spend a week or so becoming aware of the actions you take and the statements you make in reference to your classroom responsibilities. Write them down as you catch yourself making them and sort them into two categories: Proactive and Reactive. This is the first step to establishing yourself as a more proactive teacher.

Introduction

According to Harry Wong (1998), "What you do on the first days of school will determine your success or failure for the rest of the school year. You will either win or lose your class on the first day of school" (3).

There is a well-known children's song that compares the choices of two men, one very wise and the other very foolish, who set out to build houses for themselves. The wise man built his house on the rock and the foolish man built his house on the sand. When the rains came down and the floods came rushing up, the house on the rock stood firm while the house on the sand collapsed. This song illustrates the importance of having a solid foundation upon which to build and provides a metaphor representing the structures teachers must put in place if they are to be successful in their teaching endeavors.

In the classroom, the rain will come down. It is inevitable. However, if classrooms are built on a solid foundation, beginning before and continuing after the children walk through the door, the classroom will stand firm. As children cross the threshold of the classroom, it is imperative that teachers work aggressively and continuously to establish the conditions necessary for effective teaching and learning.

"What we have learned is that well-managed classrooms exist because teachers have clear ideas of the types of classroom conditions and student behaviors necessary for a healthy learning environment. They not only have clear ideas, they work to create these conditions" (Everston, Emmer, and Worsham 2003, ix). These conditions include the optimal instructional practices provided through the gradual release of responsibility model of instruction and through proactive and ongoing classroom management practices. A well-managed classroom does not just happen. It is organized and maintained through the conscious and ongoing efforts of an effective teacher.

General Beliefs About Intermediate Students

"Good management, like good teaching, is a matter of solving problems and helping people do their best" (Kohn 1993, 16). It is the responsibility of good teachers to do just that.

One component of effective instruction is working with small groups of children. In their efforts to manage small groups successfully, the number one question teachers often ask is "But, what about the rest of the class?" Inherent to answering that question is an investigation of generalized beliefs about teaching and learning. What teachers actually do when engaged in the act of teaching is motivated by what they believe about learners and the processes that underlie learning (Cambourne 1988). This leads to two questions that teachers need to ask continually in both their planning and instruction (Platt 1996):

- **Why am I doing this?**
- **How is it good for children?**

Introduction

To answer the preceding questions, teachers must first recognize some common beliefs about children and learning. Such beliefs often grow out of teachers' own experiences, but the following are some generalized beliefs about children:

- **Intermediate students want to be successful learners.**
  "A child does not have to be especially motivated or rewarded for learning, in fact, the thrust to learn is so natural that being deprived of the opportunity to learn is aversive. Children will struggle to get out of situations where there is nothing to learn" (Smith 1985, 89).

- **Intermediate students are always learning.**
  "Learning is what children do best, and under the right conditions they do so easily" (Sharon Taberski 1996 citing Bruner).

- **Intermediate students get better at whatever they practice.**
  "Practice makes perfect" is a well-known and universal saying. However, it may not always be for the best. "Asking children to take one practice test after another might reinforce ineffective test-taking strategies" (Calkins 1998, 70).

- **Intermediate students seek order.** (Note: *Order* is markedly different than *control*.)
  "But to say that children need structure or guidance is very different from saying they have to be controlled" (Kohn 1993, 32–33).

- **Intermediate students are developing a desire for and an ability to work independently.**
  "Far more than primary children, intermediate students can be independent, manage their own learning, and follow their interests" (Fountas and Pinnell 2001, 3).

- **Intermediate students experience significant social change.**
  "…they have become much more social ... Their peers are rapidly becoming more interesting—and probably more influential—than the adults in their lives" (Fountas and Pinnell 2001, 4).

In relation to the beliefs about children, the following beliefs about management and behavior emerge:

- **Intermediate students will function within whatever parameters are (or are not) set for them.**

- **Intermediate students work to be successful. If they are required to engage in a task that is too difficult or frustrating, they will work to be successful in other endeavors (e.g., disrupting the classroom, becoming the class clown, etc.).**

- **Intermediate students are strongly social beings, and their learning environment needs to respect and reflect that.**

- **Intermediate students need to be privileged with decisions and choices to make.**

- **Intermediate students are unique and individual beings. Each one is different, and his or her learning needs to be supported according to those differences.**

Introduction

- **Intermediate students may not necessarily be learning what their teachers think they are teaching.**

- **Intermediate students get better at whatever they practice. If misbehavior is practiced, students get better at misbehaving.**

The set of beliefs that teachers hold about teaching and learning drives the instructional decisions they make. If those decisions are good ones, they lead to the establishment of a solid foundation that is absolutely necessary for optimal learning to occur. In his book *The Process of Education*, Jerome Bruner quotes one of his peers who states explicitly, "When you teach well, it always seems as if 78 percent of the students are above the median" (1960). Reflective teachers must consider the alternative to such teaching: Could poor teaching possibly result in 78 percent of students functioning below the median? The primary responsibility of teachers is to coordinate an environment that is most conducive to successful teaching and learning. Just as the wise man built his house upon the rock, the classroom foundation must be thoughtfully structured so that it too will stand firm.

Building a Solid Foundation

Returning to the wisdom of Harry Wong and the metaphor presented at the beginning of the introduction, when it comes to effective literacy instruction, it is in every teacher's best interest to follow the steps of the wise man who built his house upon the rock. It is crucial for teachers to take the time to build a solid foundation based on good classroom management before venturing on to more academic pursuits.

An effective classroom is built on many firmly rooted structures and routines. In an effective classroom, the teacher will take a considerable amount of time to address the basic organization of the structures of the classroom, ranging from the organization of materials and space to the use of time to assessment and assessment practices. It is also critical that the teacher spend sufficient time initially and in an ongoing fashion to establish the routines of the classroom. A classroom is a crowded place full of materials, children, teachers, and opportunities to learn. These must be recognized and embraced to build a fully functional foundation.

Reflecting on yourself as a successful learner puts you in a proper frame of reference to explore what effective teaching is all about. "In an ideal world, if you wanted to become competent in something you did not know, you would seek an expert teacher who could give you a great deal of personal attention ... taught this way, you would ... become competent in a reasonable amount of time" (Glasser 1993, 85). Over time, an expert teacher supports learners in acquiring new skills, strategies, understandings, and behaviors through a gradual release of responsibility from teacher to learner (see the Gradual Release of Responsibility Model). Professionals such as Brian Cambourne (1988), Don Holdaway (1979), Ellin Oliver Keene (1997), and Margaret Mooney (1990) address, in their own ways, the gradual release of responsibility theory, which supports a learner as he or she gradually

Introduction

Gradual Release of Responsibility

Teacher Responsibililty DECREASES OVER TIME...

Modeled Instruction | Shared Instruction/ Joint Practice | Small Group Reading Instruction/ Supported Practice | Independent Practice

Student Responsibililty INCREASES OVER TIME...

Adapted from Pearson, P. D. and Gallagher, M. C. 1983. The instruction of reading comprehension. *Contemporary Educational Psychology*, 8, 317–344.

works to take on new learning. Each also recognizes the role of the teacher in determining where each learner is on the developmental learning curve as well as determining the best manner in which to support the continued progress of that learner.

Some key points to consider when incorporating the gradual release of responsibility into your model of classroom management and instruction include the following:

- It is important to recognize that all of the stages in the gradual release of responsibility are critical to nearly all learning opportunities, and are all necessary across the grade levels. Children at the intermediate grade levels are often far more advanced than their primary peers, but this is not always the case. Students functioning below grade level require differentiated learning opportunities that often include more modeling and scaffolded instruction than their classmates. It is also critical to recognize, though, that even if a student is functioning on or above grade level, he or she is still learning new skills and strategies and deserves the same privileges we extend to primary students: **modeling and scaffolded instruction are essential at all levels of learning, not just at the primary levels.**

- If a student is struggling to apply a skill or strategy, it is the teacher's responsibility to consider the gradual release of responsibility model to determine how to proceed next. Is more modeling required? Additional scaffolded instruction? More explicit instruction? Providing more practice is rarely the answer. **If a child is struggling with a concept, additional practice may simply more deeply ingrain their frustrations, difficulties, and improper strategy application.** It is possible to get better at doing something wrong!

Introduction

- The teacher has an important and active responsibility during the independent practice stage. As children work to apply and use the skills, strategies, and concepts they have learned, **the teacher has a responsibility to actively monitor students' efforts so that appropriate follow-up can occur,** whether in the form of extension or remediation.

- **All students are not functioning at the same level. If we expect or assume them to be at the same point on the learning continuum in any discipline, we are disrespectful of our learners and the learning process.** In reading and writing, as well as in behavior and other content areas, "it's helpful for any teacher to understand the full continuum of student development ... we would not expect all students to exhibit grade-level expectations" (Fountas and Pinnell 2001, 6). As hard as it may be for us to accept this, we must recognize that all of our students are not the same, and they deserve to be supported at whatever point on the developmental learning continuum they happen to be.

Generally, the gradual release of responsibility theory has been applied to the instruction of reading and writing. The value of this model of teaching and learning also needs to be recognized in relation to developing an effective learning environment. A teacher needs to take into account the fact that students need time and support to take on the responsibility necessary to operate successfully within the classroom.

Effective Instruction Begins with Classroom Management

It is only after the solid foundation of classroom management has been established that effective literacy instruction can begin. Effective teachers of reading and writing who are familiar with the natural learning model embodied by the gradual release of responsibility theory have grown comfortable in the knowledge that to acquire a new skill or strategy, learners need to be provided with a scaffolded form of instruction wherein the new skill is modeled for them, then approached in a shared fashion with the help of a more knowledgeable individual, then attempted by the learner in a supportive environment (Mooney 1990). The benefits of adopting the gradual release of responsibility theory should be recognized both within the establishment of a well-managed classroom and as a healthy and universally successful model for literacy teaching and learning.

In solid literacy instruction, as with all instruction, successful teachers embrace the gradual release of responsibility theory and bring it to life within their classrooms through the use of effective instructional strategies that fall into the following categories. As you read the following section, consider the value of

- **whole group instruction,**

- **small group instruction,** and

- **independent practice**

   within each content area that you teach.

Whole Group Instruction

Here are some specific examples and considerations for whole group instruction in the intermediate classroom.

Reading

Whole group instruction in reading at the intermediate level takes place in many forms, a few of which include read alouds, shared reading, and reading-related mini-lessons.

In many schools, the value of shared and modeled reading have taken on unfortunate, negative reputations at the intermediate level. When one considers the gradual release of responsibility model, this belief becomes an impossible one to hold, and the opposite—the absolute necessity for modeled and shared reading—stands out quite clearly. As children develop as readers, there is always something new to learn and, therefore, always a benefit to modeling. Sarah and Lisa each have a story to attest to this.

Sarah recalls a middle school classroom she was in that went through a remarkable transformation every day, immediately following lunch. Sarah vividly remembers the chaos of her pre-adolescent middle school experiences that seemed to simply melt away on a daily basis as her teacher pulled out a carefully selected book and bathed her students in the words of the author. Through this teacher's inclusion of a read aloud at the middle school level, Sarah was able to journey to such places as Amsterdam during the time of Nazi rule and was able to live alongside Anne Frank, coming to know and understand her world better than she would have been able to had Sarah been required to read the text on her own. In this case, the content of the text became more accessible and an entirely new genre was opened to Sarah.

As a middle and high school student, Lisa was not exposed to read alouds by her teachers. As a result, her ability to successfully navigate certain texts, even today, as a proficient reader of a great range of literature, is limited in some areas. Lisa remembers being assigned texts written by Shakespeare in both middle school and high school. Along with each assignment at each grade level came the reminder that Shakespeare's chosen model of writing was inclusive of something called "iambic pentameter." At that time, her understanding of iambic pentameter was something to the effect of "it looks like a poem, but doesn't rhyme or sound like one, so don't try to read it that way." Although this was pretty clearly impressed upon her mind, because she had no *model* for how to read Shakespeare—none of her teachers actually took the time to read it aloud in class so that Lisa could actually hear what it sounded like—to this day, as Lisa encounters a Shakespearian text, she still tries to read it as if it were a lilting, sing-song nursery rhyme. The important reminders here are: "assigning is not teaching" and "modeling is an invaluable instructional resource."

Introduction

In her book, *In the Company of Children*, Joanne Hindley also makes a point about reading aloud. Early on, Joanne valued read aloud time as an opportunity to share books with children that they could not read independently. She has since realized that "by doing all the choosing, [she] was disregarding many of the children in [her] classroom and, in fact, even hampering their ability to choose appropriate literature to read on their own" (Hindley 1996, 88). What Joanne learned has relevance for all of us. In selecting read alouds, we need to make sure that we are demonstrating that we value books that are written below, as well as those above and beyond, the actual grade level.

> We try to create communities in our classrooms where children can feel safe being who they are. But once third grade hits, it's difficult not to compare oneself to the next guy. Children want to do what their friends do, read what their friends read, regardless of how difficult this makes the job for themselves. Many of my students were choosing the books their friends were reading. I kept nudging them in other directions but without much success. We need to realize that we send strong messages about what we consider good literature with the books we choose to read out loud. As much as I wanted my students to know it was absolutely acceptable to read Rylant's *Henry and Mudge* and Reilly Giff's The Polk Street Kids series, which I consider wonderful for more "transitional" readers, I had never selected those texts for read aloud time! Once I did, and students knew we could have wonderful booktalks about these stories, I started to see more of them in children's hands during reading workshop.
> (Hindley 1996, 88)

Similar to confusions about read alouds at the intermediate level are confusions about shared reading. Many teachers automatically equate shared reading instruction with using big books. This is untrue. Shared reading instruction is an opportunity for a teacher to engage in instruction with a text that all students can see that is at a level wherein the teacher takes on greater responsibility for the reading than the students do. Using this definition, shared reading is obviously not limited to using a big book. Shared reading can incorporate any text that can be visible by all involved students. Consider using class sets of textbooks or trade books, magazines or newspapers, classroom charts, photocopies of text, or overhead transparencies of text samples. The possibilities here are nearly endless!

Writing

Similar to reading, there is great value in whole group writing instruction that far exceeds the value of merely assigning writing to students. Whole group writing instruction can include such instructional activities as mini-lessons, modeled writing done by the teacher, or shared writing, in which the students actively participate.

> *I experienced the importance of modeled writing long before I became a teacher myself, but did not recognize it until I was able to reflect on my inefficiency as a writer. As an intermediate student, I vividly remember being assigned research papers. The topic would be assigned or chosen, depending upon the teacher, and the assignment laid out: "On X date, you need to have your research paper finished. You need to turn in your note cards, your outline, and your paper together." There must have been some instruction as to what the note cards and outline were all about, because I managed to do them, but without a model, something was lost for me in the process. No matter how much time we were given, I would settle down 1–2 days before the paper was due with a stack of books and encyclopedias and would simply start typing the paper. When I found something interesting, I would add that in, but I imagine my papers were pretty similar to the format followed by the World Book Encyclopedia. As soon as I completed the paper—no small task given the fact that I did them by hand or on a typewriter since we did not have computers at the time—I would then take my paper and dutifully pull the first sentence of every paragraph to form the outline, and then created my set of note cards using the topic sentences with details from the paragraph on the back of each card. Although I did well and received great praise on how well matched each component was, the process completely eluded me since I had been provided no model. Think how much more efficient and effective I would have been as a writer if one of my teachers had modeled the steps in order, demonstrating how collecting information on note cards would allow me to easily compare and contrast multiple sources; structure an outline physically, easily noting gaps to be filled; and, ultimately, result in a paper that would virtually write itself. The importance of modeling reminds me of the new cheese commercials that are out: "Ahhhhh! The power of cheese!" Of course, in this case, it would be: "Ahhhhh! The power of modeling." —Lisa*

Content Areas

Do not forget the importance of extending the gradual release of responsibility model to all areas of instruction. The value of this model may be most readily apparent in art, music, and physical education classes where most teachers would not even think of teaching a new skill without first providing a demonstration!

Specific to reading in the content areas, students at the intermediate level sometimes struggle heavily with content area textbooks, and rightfully so! In most of their academic careers thus far, they have not been exposed to such texts, so how can we consider it fair to ask them to manage such texts now? Nonfiction texts, especially those written as textbooks, typically have a very different tone and feel to them than other books students have been exposed to. If we expect our students to successfully navigate such texts, it is our responsibility to support them to do so. If they are unable to manage the text, how on earth can they access the content within?

Introduction

An inexpensive way of securing content-specific materials is to begin collecting free pamphlets and brochures from multiple sources. Call the tourism offices for states in different parts of the country and request copies of their pamphlets. Seek them out when you are in hotels, airports, and at highway rest stops. This is an endless source of high-interest resources that are free of charge.

Management and Organization

Take care not to underestimate the role that whole group instruction can play in classroom management and organization, extending beyond announcing guidelines and routines to be adopted or followed. Modeling and role-playing appropriate actions and behaviors is invaluable.

It is also crucial that intermediate teachers seriously consider the model they themselves provide for the students in their classrooms. Children watch our interactions with other students, teachers, and parents with critical eyes. We learn from the company we keep, and the classroom teacher's behavior is something students note in all situations. Be sure that your behaviors match or exceed the expectations you hold for your students.

Small Group Instruction

As stated above, whole group instruction is *efficient*, but it is not necessarily the most *effective* model of instruction. This is why a balance between whole group and small group instruction is imperative in an effective classroom. Small group instruction provides teachers with the opportunity to group students according to their needs or abilities in order to provide instruction that is more finely tuned to children's specific needs. Since it is needs-based, small group instruction may not occur with the same frequency and for the same duration for every child in the classroom. As a matter of fact, it should not! Children have varying needs, and different students get more "mileage" out of instruction. Every student has the right to appropriate instruction, but that will most probably not come in the form of equal time. Some groups may meet frequently for short amounts of time; other groups may meet less frequently for greater amounts of time. Some students may even fall into more than one group, depending on their needs. Some "groups" may end up being a group of only one student, temporarily, again based on the needs of the learner. Small group instruction is a crucial component of an effective instructional program, and time must be found for this important component, especially in settings wherein children have different teachers for different subject areas. It is far too easy for children to get "lost in the shuffle" in such situations. Incorporating small group instruction into the overall instructional model is one way of working to ensure that all children's needs are met.

If there are students in your classroom who receive reading instruction through a Title 1 program or other similar remediation model, it is important that you also pull those children for small group instruction. As a matter of fact, when you are planning, these students should take priority. As the classroom teacher who spends the entire day with those students, you have the most opportunities to follow up on, clarify, and revisit teaching points made during small group instructional opportunities. If reading instruction is left solely up to a specialist, the potential benefits to the student may actually decrease. One of the primary benefits of additional reading instruction is that it is supplemental in nature to that of the regular classroom. In addition to quality, it is largely the additional time spent in appropriate needs-based instruction that results in the acceleration of struggling students' reading development.

Here are some specific examples and considerations for small group instruction in the intermediate classroom.

Reading

Small group reading instruction can include such events as literature circles, guided reading, mini-lessons, or book talks. In each of these examples, the children in each group are carefully selected for a very specific reason, either according to need or ability, or some combination of the two. In small group reading instruction geared to match the student's level, it is expected that the child be responsible for 90 percent or more of the reading task, including comprehension. The teacher is available to support and redirect, minimally.

Ability leveled reading groups can be categorized by the following labels that are correlated with text levels established by Fountas and Pinnell (2001): emergent (A–B), early (C–I), early fluent or transitional (J–M), and fluent (N+). Needs-based groups can be organized according to whatever observations the classroom teacher makes that lead to logical categorizations. For example, a group of students struggling to make inferences can be formed. Each can be reading a different book on a different level, with the tie that binds the group together being the common need to improve their ability to make inferences.

Writing

The purpose and value of small group writing instruction closely parallels that of small group reading instruction.

In *guided writing*, you pull together small temporary groups of writers and teach the craft, strategies, and skills those writers need at that particular time. Group work may focus on developing specific writing skills and strategies (forming paragraphs, for example), on using writing as a tool for inquiry, on learning to write in different genres, or on using technology to publish writing. The areas you focus on in guided writing are exactly the same as those in independent writing, except that you are working with a small group instead of with individuals. The groups may be convened either by you or by students who have determined on their own that they need help in a certain area or genre and have requested to be part of a group. (Fountas and Pinnell 2001, 51–52)

Content Areas

Small group instruction in the content areas serves as a helpful extension of whole group instruction. Given the fact that all students in any classroom come with varying background knowledge, it is logical that content instruction should be differentiated in a manner that supports those differences. An easy way of doing so is by providing small group instruction for ELL students, special education students, academically advanced students, or any other unique group with an opportunity to learn at their specific point along the continuum.

With advanced students, this provides an opportunity for appropriate extension and enhancement of the general curriculum. With ELL or special education students, this may take the form of review lessons, or better yet, at times through a *preview* lesson. In a preview lesson students are exposed to the concepts and content that the rest of the group will be exposed to in the near future. The lesson can be nearly identical to the one that will be provided for the entire group, but the preview will allow these students the opportunity to engage with and actively participate in the small group lesson where they will not be overshadowed by their peers, as well as in the whole group lesson in the future. For some of them, this may be the first time they have actually had the experience in a whole group lesson of having the background knowledge relevant to the lesson being taught.

Management and Organization

Generally, instruction and support related to behavior and management come in the form of whole group instruction beforehand, and whole group or one-on-one follow-up afterwards, if there is any trouble. Consider the possibility of being proactive in your management efforts and engaging in small group instruction related to behavior. It is usually a relatively small group of students that are the source of challenges within a classroom, rather than the entire group. Why not recognize this and work with the students in your classroom that you can predict will need extra time and support in order to develop self-managing behaviors? Working with small groups of students to develop these skills, as opposed to waiting until after trouble strikes, is well worth the time and energy involved.

Independent Practice

Independent practice is a necessary component to all learning. How can you ever hope to hone your skills and improve if you do not practice? An opportunity to work independently at the appropriate level is imperative for students so that they do not become bored or careless in their efforts, or become frustrated and overwhelmed. (You may have noticed that students who are required to spend time engaged in tasks that are below their independent level often become bored or careless, and students who are required to spend time on tasks that are beyond their independent capabilities often become frustrated and overwhelmed.) Other unintended consequences of pairing children with independent tasks that are beyond their current abilities include misbehavior and cheating.

Introduction

Application and practice are essential, but in order for them to be effective, they must be well-matched to the abilities of the students. This requires two things: (1) an awareness on the teacher's part of the range of abilities within the classroom, and (2) the subsequent organization of available independent activities to choose from that match that range of needs. Sometimes, practice and application take place on tasks that are even far below a student's current academic level. Practice that is "hard" is rarely most conducive to learning. Practice opportunities need to be inherently and logically tied to the learning task at hand. They need to be authentic and realistic, not contrived, artificial tasks.

Teachers have an important responsibility during this time, too. As children work independently, the teacher needs to take the time to monitor progress, behaviors, strengths, and challenges in order to best format the current and future instruction of that child.

Here are some specific examples and considerations for independent practice in the intermediate classroom.

Reading

Independent reading time, as in all independent practice, is an opportunity for students to develop and hone the skills and strategies they have been working on in whole and small group instruction. In order for students to be successful here, it is important to ensure that there is an appropriate range and volume of quality texts, in terms of quantity, type, genre, and level. Texts must also be organized and routines established such that students have easy and constant access to independent reading texts. Chapter 7 has specific ideas and suggestions for the organization of classroom libraries.

Independent reading time is primarily a time for the *student*s to be reading. Some teachers choose to use this time to read themselves, claiming that they are modeling good reading behaviors for their students. This certainly makes sense, but take care to stop "modeling" this behavior once your students no longer require a model. Your time can be much better spent interacting with individual or small groups of students as the rest read independently. Also, if you are "modeling" appropriate independent reading behavior and find yourself constantly reprimanding and redirecting students, you are being given a pretty clear sign that your demonstration is not effective, and you need to go back and re-investigate the routine.

Once a smoothly running independent reading routine has been established, the teacher's active responsibility switches to one of monitoring individual student reading behaviors. It is at this point that teachers are able to engage with individual students in order to determine future instructional needs and grouping.

Writing

Parallel to independent reading is independent writing. This is an opportunity for students to practice their developing writing skills in a comfortable environment. Much of the writing done during independent writing will never come to full publication. Sometimes, it is reviewed once, and then never again. Writers develop over *time*, not over a *piece*, and instruction needs to reflect that. Every time a child writes, he is learning something about

Introduction

being a writer. Independent writing time is a perfect time for the teacher to engage in individual writing conferences as described in Chapter 3. What the teacher learns through these conferences becomes the foundation for future whole group and small group lessons, as well as for that individual child. Students who struggle with independent writing, continually asking, "How much do we have to write?" or complaining "I don't know what to write about" are sending a message to their teacher: They are in need of mini-lessons and modeling dedicated to these topics. Simply assigning a topic or a page number would only result in further dependency and a weakening of the writer.

Content Areas

Independent work efforts in the content areas allow students of all levels to further explore a specific interest or inquiry they have relative to the general content area being studied. This may take the form of a special project, additional research, or the construction of an experiment or other model allowing them to deepen their understanding of some aspect of the content area being investigated.

Management and Organization

Just as in academic areas, children should not be punished for not knowing or demonstrating a skill related to self-managing or independent behavior. An inability or choice not to behave properly has an underlying reason, and it is the teacher's responsibility to determine what the rationale for that behavior is. It is often a result of poor initial guidance or support, in which case the fault for misbehavior lies with the teacher, not the student. In either case, the teacher takes the responsibility for reteaching or modeling the behavior in question just as would happen in any other academic area. Under the watchful eyes of an effective teacher, misbehavior rarely occurs and when it does, it is recognized as an opportunity to *teach* something, rather than to punish a child.

Within any classroom, there is a range of learners with varied needs. This is especially true in intermediate classrooms where any given teacher might have students ranging in abilities from those characteristic of an early primary student, all the way to the other end of the spectrum where some students may be functioning closer to the students at the middle or high school level. As mentioned in the previous section, to meet their students' needs, teachers must, at times, engage in whole group instruction. After all, there are large numbers of students in most classrooms, and there are a number of skills and strategies that must be introduced. Within whole group instructional models, teachers have the opportunity to explore information that, for some students, will be an introduction, for some will be a review, and for others will be a reinforcement of something they are in the process of coming to understand.

Teachers also have the responsibility for providing instruction at each individual learner's point of need. At times, they may provide this instruction in small group settings and at times on a one-to-one basis. The balance between whole group, small group, and individual instruction also requires a system that allows students to be comfortable and successful in an independent fashion.

It is to this end that this book has been organized, designed, and written. Within an instructional model based on the gradual release of responsibility theory, students need opportunities to work both with and without assistance during a typical classroom day (Dorn, French, and Jones 1998). Teachers must seriously consider what to do with the rest of the class while they are working with a single child or a small group of students. Simply handing out a packet of worksheets may keep students quiet, but may lead to sloppy or inaccurate work as a result of frustration or boredom. There are far more productive tasks that are easier to plan for and monitor that students can engage in independently that are both more appealing and conducive to optimal learning. Many specific suggestions for such activities can be found in Chapter 7 of this book.

It is also important to remember that, if assigned, independent work groups should not be aligned with reading group assignments. There is nothing more boring than spending an entire school day surrounded by the same four or five students. Mixing up these groups also ensures that teachers will not have all of the struggling readers, behavior problems, and so on together during independent and small group time. Mixing groups at these times is also one of the simplest solutions to management problems.

Armed with the knowledge that the gradual release of responsibility learning theory is truly an effective one and pairing that with the assertion made by Danielson that "the best instructional techniques are worthless in an environment of chaos" (1996, 83) it makes sense for teachers to focus first on classroom management and then on academic instruction if they hope to be optimally successful in their instruction.

> **Efficiency and Effectiveness Task**
>
> ### Monitoring Use of the Instructional Models
>
> After reading this chapter and considering the value of whole group instruction, small group instruction, and independent practice within your classroom, take a week to actually monitor your typical use of each of these instructional models. Note the amount of time and a brief description of each activity within each period or content area that you spend on whole group instruction, small group instruction, and independent practice. After collecting this data for a week, evaluate the balance within your instruction. Do you need to provide more whole group instruction and modeling? More small group instruction? More independent practice that you monitor and support?

Introduction

Section Overviews

Section  Chapters 1, 2, and 3 investigate the necessity of organizing for space, time, and assessment. They help you answer the question "How can I make the most of what I have to work with?"

Section  Chapters 4 and 5 provide a detailed look at establishing routines and planning for the first, most crucial weeks of the year. It is in this window of time that the groundwork for a year's worth of success or failure is laid.

Section  Chapters 6 and 7 provide dozens of ways in which you can structure independent and small group work time.

The appendix provides blackline masters that you may photocopy or adapt to use in your classroom.

Efficiency and Effectiveness Tasks are scattered throughout the text to help you practice and reflect on the strategies in this book.

Section 1: Creating a Climate Conducive to Learning

"Fail to plan? Plan to fail!"

This contemporary proverb sums up the importance of classroom management. When it comes to planning for success in teaching and learning, three key components come to mind:

- **Organizing for space**
- **Organizing for time**
- **Organizing for assessment**

All three of these components are elements teachers must plan for. If teachers allow themselves to be limited, controlled, or overwhelmed by them, their instruction (and general disposition) will surely suffer. It is quite possible to finish nearly every school day feeling calm and refreshed, but this is not something that just happens, it is something that teachers must organize and plan for.

To create an efficient and instructionally effective environment "...you and your students need an orderly environment with minimal disruption and wasted time, leaving everyone free to concentrate on the critical tasks of learning. Carefully planned procedures help create this environment" (Danielson 1996, 20).

No matter how carefully you organize and plan the environment, though, the classroom will not run smoothly if you continue to maintain it as YOUR classroom. Teachers need to resist the lure of running their classroom as if it were a monarchy. In order to facilitate the construction of an efficient and effective classroom, it needs to be developed in a more democratic fashion. The classroom ceases to be only YOUR space and, along with the participation of your students, it becomes OUR space. "It helps if you accept that students will not necessarily enter [the] classroom equipped to work independently in an organized educational environment. You will need to teach most students the ropes" (Fountas and Pinnell 2001, 105). Working *with* your students as you plan for space, time, and assessment will set you on a sure path to the successful construction of a productive place of teaching and learning.

Chapter 1

Organizing for Space

My first classroom more closely resembled an airport runway than it did a venue for learning. I would say it was roughly 15 feet wide and 40 feet long—the back half of what used to be the stage of an auditorium. The one existing wall was a gigantic mural featuring cartoon characters, each one about 10 feet tall. The two side walls were cinder-block stairwells that, other than functioning as entryways and exits, served no purpose to anyone other than aiding the occasional parent that discovered their usefulness in observing his or her child (and me) without being seen. An unstable, towering stack of boxes containing old basals, recycled paper, and half-used art supplies ran the length of what used to be the stage front, making up the fourth and final wall, which also doubled as the front of my room. I quickly came to the realization that I needed to take control of the space I had, or it would take control of me. —Lisa

While there are some things about a classroom that teachers cannot control (the location of walls, doors, windows, plugs, and the number of students), there are many elements that teachers can control. The physical set-up of teachers' classrooms is a direct reflection of their beliefs about teaching and learning. "The organization and look of our rooms, the materials we use, and the way we structure the day send a powerful message to children and parents about our attitudes toward teaching and our expectations for our children ... Our classrooms should reflect our goals" (Taberski 2000, 33).

Classroom teachers spend a phenomenal amount of time considering every element of their classroom environment, knowing the powerful influence the emotional and physical state of the room has in organizing for optimal teaching and learning. Fountas and Pinnell have identified two aspects related to the organization of an effective learning environment that are worthy of our attention: the physical environment and the social environment (2001). Although not optimal, the physical environment can be constructed completely independent of the students, but if the social environment is not attended to jointly, the classroom has little chance of running smoothly. For that reason, when looking at a classroom, teachers should consider not only what it looks like and sounds like but also what it *feels* like.

> Your organization of space and materials contributes to the ambiance of the classroom. Think about how order and beauty contribute to a feeling of calm and confidence in any environment. (Fountas and Pinnell 2001, 91)

Chapter 1: Organizing for Space

Efficiency and Effectiveness Task

Analyzing Your Classroom Environment

Complete the following checklists to see what your classroom feels, looks, and sounds like (see the appendix for full-page blackline masters). These are questions that you can ask as you do a 360 degree virtual tour of the classroom. Standing in one place, do a complete circle, soaking up everything about the environment. Some teachers find it valuable to sit in a student desk for a different perspective or ask a peer to come in and work through the questions together. The rest of this chapter discusses each of the checklist items in detail.

How Does the Classroom Feel?
- Do I feel comfortable as I enter?
- Do I get a peaceful sense of order, or am I overwhelmed by a sense of chaos?
- Is this a place where I would enjoy spending six (give or take) hours a day? Would I want to learn here? Could I learn here?
- What appears to be important in this room?
- Is there an appropriate space for every student in the classroom?

How Does the Classroom Sound?
- Whose voices do I hear? What are they saying?
- Are the students and teachers aware of their own voices?
- How effectively can the teacher get students' attention?

How Does the Classroom Look?
- Is there a teacher's desk? If so, where is it? How and when is it used?
- How are student desks or tables organized?
- What other large furniture items are in the classroom, and how are they arranged for optimal learning and movement?
- Are there logical pathways for movement?
- Is there a floor space large enough for intimate whole group instruction?
- Is there some place for children to work quietly?
- Are materials well organized and accessible?
- Is there an overabundance of workbooks and worksheets?
- Is there a lot of unnecessary clutter?
- Are there reference tools and resources readily available? How are they being used?
- What else is on the walls?
- Is there a classroom library? How is it organized?
- Are there clearly visible surfaces available for whole group writing instruction?
- Do students have a sense of how the environment has been organized?

Section 1

How Does the Classroom Feel?

When considering the "feel" of a classroom, a teacher addresses the degree to which the learning environment is safe, comfortable, and pleasant. "Is this a place where I would want to spend several hours every day learning with and from others? Do I feel good being here?" are questions that teachers might ask when evaluating their classroom environment.

Everyone has experienced uncomfortable environments in the past—a restaurant in which you hold concerns about the cleanliness of the kitchen, an electronics store in which you are overwhelmed by the frenzied environment and the pressure of the employees to make a quick decision, or a doctor's office that does not provide a caring atmosphere but rather a rushed feeling of being another faceless individual in a never-ending list of patients. In all of these situations, you, as a customer, develop a "feel" or a "sense" as to what that business is all about. The business within a classroom is not altogether different. Take a closer look at what lies behind the following questions posed in the Efficiency and Effectiveness Task related to creating a climate conducive to learning.

> As teachers, "creating an atmosphere that encourages students to interact, feel independent, and take pride in the upkeep of their classroom is crucial for everything we do throughout the year." (Hindley 1996, 5)

Do I Feel Comfortable as I Enter?

Glasser (1993) believes that a classroom environment must be warm and supportive for quality teaching and learning to occur. It is a teacher's responsibility to organize for such an environment. The tone of a classroom envelops teachers and students the second they cross its threshold. Children know almost immediately whether they have entered a forum for learning in which they would feel comfortable making mistakes and celebrating successes. This feeling is almost tangible in some classrooms, and it is imperative that this tone is a positive one. Teachers should ask themselves, "Could I joyfully leave my child (or sibling or niece or nephew or grandchild) in this room for a day? Will he or she be loved and nurtured and come home happy and overflowing with new things to share that he or she learned that day?"

"In a good classroom, everyone counts and everyone deserves respect" (Fountas and Pinnell 2001, 96). This is another example of the almost tangible effects of a supportive learning environment. Relationships between teachers and students are not islands in a classroom. There is a powerful network connecting each and every one. If there is an awkward or counter-productive relationship between any individuals in the classroom, all other relationships in that classroom are affected. As hard as it may be, it is the teacher's responsibility as the leader to ensure that the relationships are characterized by respect. This includes the teacher's relationship with every student. When there are difficulties in a teacher-student relationship, this becomes very clear to other students who may pick up on and mirror the tension or behaviors demonstrating a lack of respect. As the adult in the classroom, the teacher must be an icon of respectful, cooperative, collaborative interactions.

Every message that is sent and every action the teacher takes is a powerful demonstration and, ultimately, a strong coercer of student behavior. What are you modeling for your children? This is tied inherently to the overall tone and feel of the classroom.

Do I Get a Peaceful Sense of Order, or Am I Overwhelmed by a Sense of Chaos?

It is much easier to learn in a place of order or one that is characterized by structure than a classroom that is ruled by chaos or a lack of attention to organization. It is important to note that there is a distinction between an orderly learning environment and one that is controlled. A classroom that is well organized and emanates a sense of promise, efficiency, and clear expectations is orderly. A classroom that is artificially controlled leaves children with an uncomfortable feeling, almost fearful of what would happen if they unknowingly violated one of the "rules."

On the other hand, some classrooms can be characterized by their utter lack of order or structure. When you enter such environments, you get the feeling that everything has been haphazardly organized, from the learners to the learning. These rooms may be loud, unruly, and chaotic.

In an effort to establish order in their classrooms, teachers must again remind themselves that there is a distinct difference between children functioning in an ordered environment, responsible for making choices about their behavior, and a teacher asserting control over the students, with little attention to students' needs as learners.

> The way in which a classroom is organized and operated teaches students every day what life in that classroom should be like. (Fountas and Pinnell 2001, 105)

Section 2 provides greater detail on how to go about establishing a teaching and learning environment that is free of chaos and disarray, and, instead, characterized by seamless order that comes about as a result of the joint efforts of the teacher and students.

I once heard an odd metaphor comparing children to fleas. Fleas, it seems, are very easy to train. You place them in a jar and cover it. The insects very quickly learn the limits of their environment and leap up, stopping just below the place where they had recently come in contact with the lid. Interestingly enough, if the lid is then removed, the fleas continue to leap up to just below where the lid used to be and no higher. They have learned their limits and continue to function within them. The comparison made to children suggests that if we can clearly define the parameters within which they are allowed to function, they will do so. I have no idea whether fleas can be trained in this manner, and I certainly do not think we should liken children to insects; however, I do believe that children do a marvelous job of functioning within the parameters we set for them. The difference between an orderly classroom and a chaotic one may very well be the difference between well-defined and logical parameters, and having poorly defined limits, or none at all. —Lisa

Section 1

Is This a Place Where I Would Enjoy Spending Six (give or take) Hours a Day? Would I Want to Learn Here? Could I Learn Here?

This item relates to the tone and the feel of the classroom. Would I want to spend time here? "The classroom is, in fact, a laboratory for social justice. It is not only multicultural; it is also antiracist" (Fountas and Pinnell 2001, 108). Brain research studies show that emotion drives learning and attention (Caine and Caine 1994). If students are in an unpleasant, unenjoyable, or threatening environment, they will downshift (Hart 1983) to the lowest form of learning—rote memorization. Rote memorization is, in effect, a survival skill: Just tell me what to do and I will do it! Others disagree with the downshifting metaphor. Instead, they believe that students' emotions intensify to put them on high alert when they feel threatened (Sylwester 1998). They react unconsciously and automatically: Act first—think later. Either way, children will not be in a state conducive to optimal learning.

> It is widely understood that people learn by example. But adults who are respectful of children are not just modeling a skill or behavior; they are meeting the emotional needs of those children, thereby helping to create the psychological conditions for children to treat others respectfully. ... It is the accumulation of such small gestures of respect that create a climate where kids are inclined to act likewise–with the teacher and with each other.
> (Kohn, 1998, p. 5)

As stated in the introduction, students want and need to learn. When they are not able to do so, they will engage in other, less-desirable behavior. If a child is faced with tasks that are too challenging, too simple, or that leave unfilled time, he or she will take the opportunity to entertain him- or herself with something that would be more engaging. Many times this takes the form of inappropriate behavior that will disallow that child and possibly other students to learn.

What Appears to Be Important in This Room?

The answer to this question provides insight into what the teacher sees as important. "What teachers actually *do* when engaged in the act of teaching is motivated by what they *believe* about the processes that underlie learning" (Cambourne 1988, 17). The decisions teachers make on a daily basis are directly influenced and guided by what they believe about the processes of teaching and learning (Cambourne 1988). Not only does instruction reflect a teacher's beliefs, the entire classroom environment becomes a product of what that teacher believes.

Reflecting on the answers to the questions about how your classroom feels (refer to the Efficiency and Effectiveness Task) will set you on the road to confirming or reorganizing your current beliefs about teaching and learning in your classroom. Determine where it is that you feel that you might need to spend more time and energy in your instruction, and then focus on that element.

Is There an Appropriate Space for Every Student in the Classroom?

This item refers to both the size and the nature of the space students occupy. It is very difficult to learn if you are uncomfortable, so intermediate teachers need to be especially sensitive to the variation of size of students in their classroom. Students may range from barely three feet tall to over six feet tall at the third through sixth grades, and a classroom teacher sensitive to the learning needs of her students will work to be respectful of each of these student's needs. "Your physical environment should be comfortable for all students, who will vary both in height and size" (Fountas and Pinnell 2001, 89).

> *On the very first day of school one year, I found that I had unknowingly placed the tallest and the shortest third grader in the school right next to each other in identical chairs and desks! With one standing at three and a half feet tall and the other at a full six feet, the difference was not something that was unnoticeable. Knowing that I had to act quickly to establish this classroom as a comfortable place for each student, both physically and emotionally, I decided to make some changes. Rather than singling out the two students, I announced to the whole class that we would all be moving around a bit today and called the entire group to the floor, suggesting that students could choose to sit on the floor or on one of the chairs at the edge of the mat. This allowed me to see what was more physically comfortable, given the choice, for each of my students. Changing my lesson plans, I read a story aloud to the group and then asked them to quietly discuss the story. As they did so, I tore to the back of the room and rearranged the spaces I had randomly chosen for each child so that many of the children's original seats were moved, but none were singled out, including the two students at the extreme ends of the height continuum. Each one found himself in a more appropriately sized desk and chair, and no longer sitting directly next to one another. —Sarah*

The nature of each student's space is also important to consider. A responsible teacher will take the time to sit in the space to be occupied by every child to consider whether that space would be conducive to learning. For example, a teacher may find a logical reason for undesirable behavior on the part of a student by merely placing herself in that student's seat. It may turn out that this seat has a perfect view into the front office, the playground, or a well-traveled hallway! In this case, a student's distraction is quite logical and reasonable. A teacher may be unable to see this from any other position in the classroom, but by placing herself in that student's space, a whole new classroom view, as well as an understanding of certain student behaviors, may suddenly become available.

Section 1

Efficiency and Effectiveness Task

What Appears to Be Important in This Room?

You may want to investigate what appears important in your room by inviting a peer to observe you or by videotaping yourself on several occasions to measure yourself more objectively.

Have your peer answer or ask yourself the questions below (see the appendix for full-page blackline masters). At the intermediate level, it may also be of interest or value to offer your students the opportunity to complete the following survey, either in its original or in a modified form.

- Where does the teacher position him- or herself for instruction?
- Is there a balance of voices in the room, or are only certain students and the teacher being heard?
- Is there an imposing feeling of control?
- Does the teacher go to the children or do the children have to go to the teacher?
- If the children go to the teacher, is there a long line of children constantly seeking help or approval?
- Is covering the content, regardless of student needs, an overshadowing characteristic?
- Physically, how are things organized?
- How does the teacher convey that books and reading are important? Are books easily accessible to students?
- How does the teacher honor children's work? Is the work visible?
- Do learners appear to be self-motivated and independent?

How Does the Classroom Look?

In his infinite wisdom, Don Holdaway (1979) maintains that "much teaching energy is spent on compensating for an unfavorable environment. It would be far more sensible to use our energies first on the environment itself" (15).

There is no one best way to organize the physical elements of a classroom. Teachers must look individually at their classrooms and the physical elements that they contain as the tools to craft instruction. Teachers must determine what they are hoping to achieve and accomplish and seriously consider how the organization of the physical environment can either help or hinder them as they take on the responsibility for doing so. A carpenter might be able to pound a nail in using a screwdriver but that would obviously not be the most efficient and effective manner in which to achieve that goal. The same is true for the decisions teachers make about how to use their classroom tools. If teachers organize materials and environments wisely in the first place, they will save countless hours and great stress as they proceed through the year. At the intermediate level, students should be actively involved in this process, establishing the classroom as a shared place to be called "home" by all. This is possible to do, even in classrooms that are characterized by groups of children rotating through them throughout the day. The following are areas of the classroom, or elements within it, that teachers should address when considering their room arrangement.

Is There a Teacher's Desk? If So, Where Is It? How and When Is It Used?

> Some years ago, Regie Routman convinced me to eliminate the teacher's desk to help convey the idea that the classroom is child-centered. I found it difficult at first. Where would I put my lesson plan book? Where would the student teacher and I pile office memos and handouts? I have compromised by using a small table that is not, as my desk was, the first thing you notice when you enter the classroom.
> (Servis 1999, 16)

You may consider following Routman's advice by getting rid of your monstrous, space-eating desk. The need for space is great enough as it is; why exacerbate the problem by having a piece of furniture that is not even (or rarely) used during the school day? The role of the teacher in any classroom is to be in the immediate presence of one, some, or all of the students. If children are reading, writing, or working independently, the teacher should be working with a small group or conferencing one on one with a student.

Obviously, the teacher's desk is a location to store important items such as office supplies, files, and plan books. However, you may consider the possibility of organizing an alternate storage system for these items that would not take up so much space. Try using a small table or a student desk. Getting rid of the desk will also help you with another issue—hanging onto unnecessary clutter. Think of all the things that end up on your desk, just because the space is there.

If you decide to keep your desk, it is best to move it to the back of the room, or an obscure corner. Then its presence does not dominate the classroom, sending the message "This is my classroom. You are here for me" as opposed to "This is our classroom, and I am here for you."

How Are Student Desks or Tables Organized?

Joanne Hindley (1996) quotes her colleague Isabel Beaton at the Manhattan New School: "Geography is everything. I realized that I needed to figure out what I wanted to happen and how my classroom geography could support and enhance—or inhibit and deter—those goals" (5).

Organizing desks in rows is a common way to organize the classroom; however, it is not the most conducive arrangement to learning. Humans are social beings and they need to talk. Talking is part of learning—it is how children solidify the information that they have acquired and best process new information as they integrate that into their existing schema. Because the social environment is closely connected to—in fact, imbedded in—the learning environment, teaching children how to get along with others is certainly an appropriate instructional practice.

Section 1

Efficiency and Effectiveness Task

Explore Different Points of View

Take the time one day to actually sit down in every place in the classroom that a child would occupy, either in whole group instruction, small group instruction, or independent practice. As you do, consider:

- How do I feel here? Am I an important part of this classroom?
- Am I comfortable here? Is there enough room for my body? How long can I sit here and still maintain my focus?
- What can I see from here? Can I see the overhead screen? The teacher? Other students' faces?
- What is there around to distract me? Am I next to the window? A door? The bathroom? Am I looking out across the hallway into another classroom? Are there computer screens catching my attention?
- How is the volume here? Can I hear clearly? Is there noise within the classroom distracting me? Is there outside noise distracting me?

What Other Large Furniture Items Are in The Classroom, and How Are They Arranged for Optimal Learning and Movement?

Many intermediate teachers have taken advantage of garage sales and extra personal furniture items and brought them into their classrooms. These teachers recognize that the standard issue student chair and desk/table may not be the most comfortable setting in which to learn. Couches, comfortable chairs, large cushions, bean bag chairs, and even old bathtubs have started to appear in classrooms, providing students with choices for where to sit so that their learning experience can be a comfortable one.

Teachers who have decided to incorporate such unorthodox furniture as couches and bean bag chairs into their classroom scheme have been overwhelmingly pleased with the effects. The classroom turns into a den of learning that is both comfortable and productive, but not without potential problems that the teacher and students must consider proactively. "We have two new bean bag chairs in the classroom. I don't think that all 26 of us can fit on them at the same time. Does anyone have an idea for how we could manage this so that it doesn't become a problem?" Consider each suggestion seriously, no matter how inane. For example, my students would suggest things like "Whoever gets there first gets it!" Instead of interjecting my thoughts, I added it to the growing list of possible ways of handling the potential problem. After we listed all the options, the students went through each. Very quickly, they came to the realization that a "First come, first served!" system would not work well in this situation, and they chose another route. In this case, they chose to post a class list that had been generated in random order. Every time a child had a turn, he or she would cross his or her name off the list and the next turn would go to the next student on the list. —Lisa

Are There Logical Pathways for Movement?

The best way to answer this question is to take a walking tour of the classroom to ensure there are appropriate pathways for movement. Also make sure that furniture and materials are organized in such a fashion that teachers and students can easily access instructional materials.

> *I unintentionally designed my first classroom with one gigantically long and narrow passage that made my travel path easier but also invited children to barrel straight across the classroom at top speed. A quick turn of a bookshelf required a few additional steps on my part but, at the same time, slowed my students down considerably—a change that was worth the minor inconvenience to me. —Lisa*

> *Last year we were struggling a lot with transitions. On a particularly bad day, it could take almost 10 minutes to get the students to switch from one activity to another. I tried giving more explicit directions. I had someone repeat the directions to me to make sure that everyone knew exactly what needed to happen. I tried timing them to make it more like a game. Nothing was working. I then made a simple classroom map on a scrap piece of paper. I wanted to find out exactly where the problems were happening. I tracked the traffic patterns for several transitions, but it only took the first one to see what was happening. There wasn't enough room to LEAVE THE MEETING AREA! The furniture made it so that only 2 or 3 kids could leave or enter the meeting area at a time. How simple! All I had to do was push the couches and the bookshelf back a few feet, and the traffic was solved. Less congestion. Less time for transitions. More time for learning. I was amazed at how a simple sketch of the classroom on the back of a piece of paper made the obvious problem come to life.*
> *—Mary Clancy; Fifth Grade Teacher; New York, New York*

Is There a Floor Space Large Enough for Intimate Whole Group Instruction?

The choice of the term "intimate" to describe this space dedicated to whole group instruction was a thoughtful one. It is easy to use student desk or seat space as the venue for whole group lessons, but oftentimes, something is lost in this more formal setting that far too easily lends itself to teacher-centered, lecture-like instruction. By organizing a more comfortable setting outside of the students' usual work space, a different learning context is created that is more conducive to focused and purposeful mini-lessons and conversations that evolve from the students' needs. In this setting, where everyone can easily see everyone else's face as the students and teacher gather together comfortably—on the floor, low benches, chairs, couches, or cushions—the classroom becomes a true community.

If teachers are going to engage in effective instructional practices and plan on generating such a classroom community, they need to organize their environment to first have adequate

Section 1

space for the group to congregate. It is possible to move furniture to make such a space, but "teachers who rearrange furniture throughout the day frequently become frustrated … it is easier in the long run to designate a section of the room as the gathering place, and then design the rest of the classroom around it" (Taberski 2000, 21). This might mean rethinking some of the items that you currently have in your classroom that are taking up space. In order to create a whole group meeting area, great changes may need to take place elsewhere.

In your own classroom, try to seek out a cozy corner for this floor space. You also might want to make sure your back is to the wall so children do not have any option other than to look at you when it is your turn to speak. If you are in front of a window or door or in the inner part of the room, children can easily find all sorts of interesting things to look at instead of focusing their attention on you and the task at hand. Also be sure that there are no distractions in children's immediate presence. If they are sitting right next to active computers or other distracting materials, they may easily find something more exciting to focus their attention on.

Once you organize your spot, choose a location for yourself. As a member of the classroom community, it is important for you to be a part of the group, but at the same time maintain a presence as the leader. Just as for your students, it is important to be comfortable, but be sure not to "throne" yourself in the classroom, reserving the best spot for yourself such that your community becomes divided from its guide and leader. Take care with your positioning of yourself. To appreciate the feel of an instructional setting where the teacher holds such a regal position, consider what it would be like if you were sitting in a workshop or college course and your instructor was standing on a chair teaching. The physical distance between a teacher and learner sends an unspoken message to the learner.

Some classrooms are so small that organizing this floor space becomes an earnest challenge. If you find that you are truly struggling to organize your classroom to accommodate floor space and have tried rearranging the furniture to no avail, you can teach children how to move minimal furniture quickly to create an instant space. If you do not have a carpeted floor, put a sliced tennis ball on each table and chair leg to reduce noise and increase ease in moving the objects; then place an "X" on the floor with tape to indicate where the furniture should be moved to and returned to. Children can rapidly slide back one or two tables and then return them to their original position as needed. It is important to use this as a last resort as every time the furniture has to be moved instructional time is wasted. If it does not seem so, estimate how long you think it takes children to rearrange the furniture a single time and then multiply that by how many times a day/week/year that would occur. The minutes add up quickly. If at all possible, it is best to secure the necessary space by organizing for it as a constant in the classroom rather than to arrange for it over and over on a regular basis.

Is There Some Place for Children to Work Quietly?

Students have the right to a working environment that will allow them to be successful. Much of this will be addressed through the guidelines and norms established for the independent work behaviors in the classroom, but it is a good idea to have an area or areas in the classroom specifically designated as peaceful work areas for children who are intensely engaged in learning tasks and do not want to be disrupted. This location might be used for independent work or work with a peer. Take care to ensure that such a location does not turn into a hiding spot or a hangout for off-task students. There are many locations that can serve dual purposes in a classroom that is short on space. For example, consider using the floor space in the classroom library as a quiet place to spread out and work. Intermediate children are quite comfortable sprawling on the floor at home. Why not let them do the same in their classroom?

Are Materials Well Organized and Accessible?

This goes for both student and teacher materials. It is easy to see how well organized a teacher is by taking a quick glance around the room. Are supplies neatly organized and labeled? Or are they piled helter-skelter, here and there? What do children's desks look like? Are they overflowing with crumpled paper and books? It is critical for teachers to have a system for themselves and their students. In establishing that system, it is wise to make use of labels, indicating where certain items are found and should be returned. Students are masterful designers and artists and inviting them to take part in labeling different materials reduces your work load and increases their engagement, responsibility, and ownership.

Arranging materials is only the first step toward organization. It is also important to teach students how to be respectful of materials. School supplies may very well be the only

> **Efficiency and Effectiveness Task**
>
> **Mapping the Classroom**
>
> After reading through all the strategies for organizing the physical classroom, use graph paper to sketch out the boundaries, doorways, locations of plugs, and other unchangeable elements within your classroom. Then use sticky notes cut to size, representing furniture and other movable items, to play with different room arrangements. Make sure to block out floor space for whole group gatherings and other work spaces, trying out as many options as necessary before deciding which one works the best.
>
> It would be an interesting and valuable activity to ask your students to do the same task, either individually, with a partner, or in a small group. It would double as a mathematics activity as well as a management strategy, requiring serious thought and reflection on the students' part. Ask them to come up with a design or model for the classroom and present it, justifying their decisions. This activity will also prove to be a powerful assessment tool for the teacher, allowing for an inside view of how different students view classroom structure and community. Look for what is prominent and valued in the designs, and you will learn a lot about your students.

Section 1

items in their world that children have the privilege of being responsible for. It is the responsibility of teachers to recognize and support them as they learn to care for and respect their materials and those belonging to others, including the teacher. It is a much easier task to accomplish if you ask children to be responsible for a minimum of items initially, and then to broaden that base as they demonstrate readiness.

> *My favorite and most productive years as a classroom teacher were the ones when I started the school year with a completely barren classroom. There was nothing on the walls, nothing on the shelves, and nothing on the tables. On the first day of school, we put a basket on each table for snacks and pencil boxes, and every child received one pencil. Later in the day, a single basket of books was introduced but that was it. Nearly every day for the rest of the year, we added items to our room, and it grew slowly over time. When the painting supplies came out of one of the boxes we had lengthy talks about the care and storage of these materials. I rarely found anything out of place these years as the classroom truly belonged to all of us.* —Lisa

Is There an Overabundance of Workbooks and Worksheets?

Jeanette Veatch (1997) once stated that if teachers ever have all of their students doing the same thing at the same time, they had better stop and have a think about what they are doing. Having all students working independently on the same type of worksheet is not beneficial in supporting learning. On any given worksheet, there may be ten to twenty items, all focusing on relatively similar tasks. If the child has done the first four or five correctly, you can pretty much assume that he or she understands the task. The rest of the worksheet would then be largely wasted time. On the other hand, if a child gets the first handful of items wrong, he or she has clearly demonstrated that he or she does not understand the task. If he or she is required to complete the worksheet, he or she will undoubtedly continue making the same errors, in effect practicing them, getting better and better at doing that task incorrectly. This is a perfect example of how using the two questions from the introduction will help you move to a more reflective practice:

- **Why am I doing this?**

- **How is it good for children?**

Many teachers have also tried to use packets of worksheets as management tools. If these resources are not multi-leveled and differentiated, they are inherently poor choices for individual work opportunities. It is far wiser to invest time and energy in establishing independent work activities that will allow children to engage with tasks that are more meaningful and are directly linked to authentic reading and writing.

If you do choose to use worksheets, be acutely critical of those that you select for use. Ask yourself for every worksheet and every child "Why am I doing this? How is it good for this child?" You may need to take it a step further and ask yourself, "How is doing this worksheet going to help this student become a better reader or writer?" If you cannot answer these questions satisfactorily, you need to find alternate activities that will support literacy development. In addition to having students simply read and write for extended periods of time, look at Section 3 for suggestions of authentic activities your students can engage in instead.

> Startling as this may sound, the truth is that many children read for a remarkably small percentage of the school day. Researchers have for a long while documented that children in many classrooms spend more time on dittoes and exercises, multiple-choice questions, and language drills than on reading whole texts. Children sometimes spend two-and-a-half hours in reading instruction and only ten minutes of that time actually reading. (Calkins, Montgomery, and Santman 1998, 51)

Is There a Lot of Unnecessary Clutter?

Teachers are notorious for being pack rats. Anything that comes their way seems to find itself a home in the classroom. Even though teachers eventually use some of it, it seems that great quantities of clutter accumulate in each classroom. Some classrooms may even have piles teetering dangerously, somewhat like Sarah Cynthia Sylvia Stout's garbage pile in Shel Silverstein's (1974) poem. There are several problems with this unnecessary accumulation. Some teachers tend to collect so much of it that when it comes time to use whatever they need, they often struggle to find it because it is buried so deeply in years' worth of collected treasures. You may have found yourself holding onto items for years on end, thinking, "But I might need it someday!" Take a close look at what you have sitting around. The classroom is a home to children for six hours or more every day. Such an overwhelming environment will surely make it harder for students to learn and definitely make it harder for you to teach. A good rule to follow: If you have not used it for a year, get rid of it.

Are There Reference Tools and Resources Readily Available? How Are They Being Used?

Intermediate students are developing increasingly independent behaviors as they become more and more responsible for their own learning. In order to support this, teachers need to organize the environment to provide the necessary resources that will allow students to function in such a manner. Such resources may include word walls designated to certain spelling patterns or other categories, dictionaries, thesauruses, encyclopedias, word study notebooks, or access to the internet. Merely making such resources available and easily accessible is not enough, however. Far too many dictionaries, reference books, computers, and word banks are grossly underutilized in classrooms because the teacher in that room has made them available, but neglected teaching students how to use them through repeated modeling.

For example, the word walls often seen in primary classrooms have an invaluable cousin that is quite appropriate at the intermediate level. The word wall should be 100 percent empty on the first day of school. That is right—100 percent empty. *Teaching Reading and*

Writing with Word Walls: Easy Lessons and Fresh Ideas for Creating Interactive Word Walls That Build Literacy Skills (Wagstaff 1999) is full of suggestions for variations on word walls. Wagstaff reminds teachers that a word wall should look different in every classroom and will never look the same from year to year, as it needs to be designed and crafted to meet the unique set of needs being represented in that classroom. At the intermediate level, such a word wall may center on certain orthographic or etymological structures, or may even be a content-related resource bank.

No matter the content, a word wall needs to be located in clear view of the space where modeled and shared writing will occur, and it also needs to be visually accessible to students as they are writing independently. The teacher has a responsibility in modeling how to use this resource on a daily basis. One final concern about word walls relates to the words that make their way onto them: Be hyper-vigilant as to what words appear there, choosing those that will be of greatest benefit to students as they write and spell. Placing every word that children would ever want or need to spell or use on the wall would be ridiculous. The only result would be ultimate dependency on the wall as a word bank. Certainly some words can be used in this manner, but most of the words appearing on the wall should be there to provide links or connections to other words. "Curious whether or not your word walls are effective? Evaluate honestly whether or not students are using them in everyday reading and writing" (Routman 2003, 210).

> As part of minilessons, you can create wall charts that illustrate principles and provide a place for students to list examples. These wall charts become ready references for the kinds of generalizations that students are exploring, and they illustrate the value of constantly searching for connections. (Fountas and Pinnell 2001, 377)

Efficiency and Effectiveness Task

Evaluating Classroom Reference Tools and Resources

Take some time to evaluate the reference tools and resources in your classroom. Ask yourself the following questions:

- What resources are available to my students?
- How were those resources introduced?
- Do I refer to them frequently through my own modeled use of them, or do I simply direct students to use them without repeated demonstration of their purpose and use?
- Do my students use the resources I have made available?
- What could I do to ensure that they are utilized?

What Else Is on the Walls?

Most teachers are familiar with the "Hang in there!" poster with a kitten hanging off a branch. It is cute and has a positive message, but most struggling students do not look up, gather energy from that cat, and think, "If he can do it, I can do it!" When walls are filled with posters like this one, they merely serve as wallpaper. "It is important that child-made charts be at least as numerous as those made by teachers" (Cambourne 1988, 46).

The best resources to cover the classroom walls are large chart papers filled with texts you have created for or jointly with students. They provide meaningful examples that will support students as they incorporate in their own writing the same strategies you visited as a group.

> *After spending a few days working on a text, I told my students that I was so proud of their efforts that I was going to hang their (unedited) work on the wall outside of the classroom. About half of the kids were thrilled and the other half could care less. I will never forget one student exclaiming, "But Ms. D., it's wrong! I spelled it all wrong. Don't hang it. It's wrong!" I was working so hard to make the point that I accepted her effort that I completely violated her as a learner. As I posted her work for all to see, she was mad at me and embarrassed—and rightfully so. Up to that point, she was happily taking risks and making mistakes, but when I displayed that to the world, I lost her trust. I certainly could have edited her work to make it perfect and then hung it up, but I did not think that would be fair, either. The only message that would have sent would be "You're not a very good writer, but look at what a great editor I am." I believe that we need to honor children's work, but I am not sure that I have to post their efforts publicly to do that. How would you feel if you were the poorest writer in the room and that fact was publicized weekly? I shudder at the thought of one of my college professors taking one of my essays and stapling it outside his door—no matter how good or bad. Why do it to children? —Lisa*

So what is the best approach when hanging student work? Should teachers edit everything, make it perfect, and then post it? Or, should teachers post less than perfect student work that might advertise incorrect writing elements? Irene Fountas and Gay Su Pinnell had the same questions and share the following wisdom: "The vast majority of work that is published in a classroom can be jointly constructed text that comes from shared or interactive writing lessons. Some of it can come from modeled writing that you do, and a portion should be children's independent writing" (Fountas and Pinnell 1996, 46).

> Since much of the print on display surfaces will serve as reading material, the print should be in standard spelling. Children will use approximated spellings as they construct words in their journals and independent writing, and these may be labeled to honor children's work. Teachers can label these as "works in progress" to distinguish them from published work. (Fountas and Pinnell 1996, 46)

Similar to Fountas and Pinnell's suggestion of noting "works in progress," you might create an entire bulletin board dedicated to housing all of the odds and ends of writing samples that students want to post. Students will be thrilled to be "published," and you can take comfort knowing that this is self-selected participation. It is important to note that this bulletin board serves as a celebration, not as a writing resource. If you are seeking simple ways to do this, divide a bulletin board into even spaces, each one with a student's name in it, and provide a set of thumbtacks to allow each student to fill his or her space as he chooses. Or, you might post large resealable bags labeled with each student's name. The student is allowed to choose whatever he or she would like to put into the resealable bag as a celebration of his or her work.

Efficiency and Effectiveness Task

What Is on Your Walls?

Fill out the chart at the right (see the appendix for a full blackline master). As you go through your day, circle the items your students use or attend to regularly. Star the items you model the use of. After about a week, review your list and decide which materials on your walls are valuable instructional materials and which need to go.

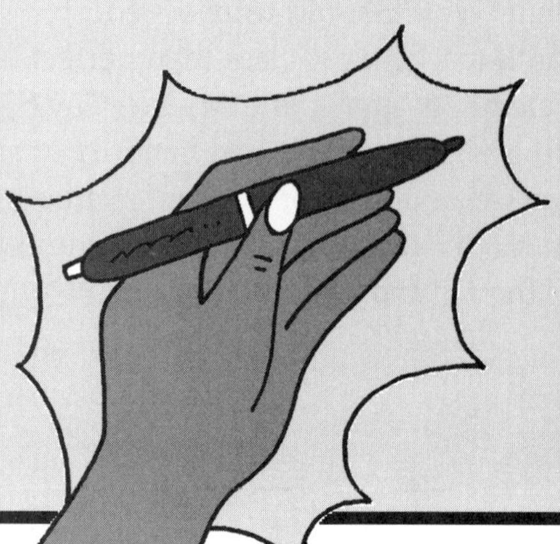

What Is on Your Walls?

Fill out the following chart. As you go through your day, circle the items your students use or attend to regularly. Star the items you model the use of. After about a week, review your list and decide which materials on your walls are valuable instructional materials and which need to go.

Items I Purchased	Things I Made

Things I Made With My Students	Things My Students Made

Is There a Classroom Library? How Is It Organized?

The best way to organize the classroom library is the way that is going to benefit you and your students directly; however, you may find that in looking to the experts (such as the Barnes and Noble and Borders bookstores), you can learn a lot. Their texts are largely organized by category and, sometimes, by level of difficulty, such as the Children's and Young Adult's sections, but for the most part, the reader is responsible for deciding which book is most appropriate for him or her. Whichever system you choose, make sure to review the system with students so they can put the books away correctly.

If you choose to organize your classroom library into categories, you might start with baskets organized by award categories such as Newbery books, by topics such as animals or science, by author collections such as R.L. Stine, or by genre. The following is a suggested list of categories:

Classroom Library Possible Categories:

Art and Painting	Geography	Mysteries	Science Fiction
Biographies	History	Newbery Winners	Series
Countries	Holidays	Novels	Spanish
Favorite Authors	Math	Poetry	Sports
Food	Music	Science	

If you have not organized your classroom library before, to save time and to include your students in the process, do not try to sort and categorize all the books yourself. If you have hundreds of books, this could take several weekends that could be better spent doing many other things that have nothing to do with school! Instead, elicit the help of your students. You might suggest, "Hey, I have a basket here for all of our Newbery books. If you see one while you're reading this week, please pull it out and put it in the basket marked 'Newbery Award Winners.'" For the next week or so, your students will do all the work, and then you can look for another category. This method may take longer, but the benefits will outweigh the time factor. Being responsible for the sorting results in students being more responsible for returning books to their appropriate basket in the long run.

To maintain the organization of the books, place a sticker on each basket with a matching sticker on each book. For example, the books about plants may all have a tree sticker. You may decide to take care to introduce the books in your library slowly and over time rather than all at once. Add only a small selection of books each week, gradually building up the library to aid students rather than overwhelm them.

Be careful when organizing your books if you are considering leveling them. Leveled books are appropriate for instruction, not so much for free reading opportunities. While it is important to ensure that students are regularly reading and applying their developing strategy base to books they can read independently, it may be a mistake to narrow children's selections to only books at a certain level. One reason for this is that there are times when readers desire to and should read either below or above their reading level. As adults, we do it all the time. I regularly find myself matched with texts that I am highly interested in, but that are out of reach of my current reading abilities. In such cases, as a proficient reader, I am knowledgeable enough to call on strategies that will allow me to be successful with such texts. Similarly, we often find ourselves reading texts well below our reading level as we pick up popular books, magazines, or even children's books. Each of these has a purpose in our lives as readers.

Establishing broad categories of levels may be helpful, but, more importantly, for children struggling to choose appropriate texts, mini-lessons need to be conducted to assist them to do so on their own. Giving a child a book on his or her reading level will ensure an appropriate match between text and reader, but it will not help the child learn to choose books at an appropriate level on his or her own. This skill is a necessary one, and a responsible teacher will work to help students learn how to do this rather than construct the environment so that the decision is made by the teacher. If you don't plan on following your students around for the rest of their lives, indicating which books are appropriate, don't teach them to be dependent upon you to do so!

Are There Clearly Visible Surfaces Available for Whole Group Writing Instruction?

In an intermediate classroom, the best surfaces for whole group writing instruction are either overhead projectors or sturdy easels with either white boards or paper to write on. Traditional wall-mounted chalkboards do not provide an optimal instructional situation. Whole group writing activities are intimate teaching and learning opportunities that require consistent eye contact with learners. If you are writing on a wall-mounted board, every time you write, you have to turn completely and put your back to your students' faces. This makes it impossible for you to recognize nods of understanding or points of confusion that will require further attention in your instruction—you cannot read the eyes and faces of students if your back is to them. If you write on the overhead projector or a slanted surface that you sit or stand next to, you can maintain eye contact for a majority of the instructional time, and then just shift your gaze to the paper when necessary.

One of the best writing surfaces, of course, is the overhead projector. An overhead projector allows you to write in a normal fashion, more true to size, and maintain near constant eye contact with your audience. One of the most successful uses of the overhead projector is when it is flat on the floor rather than on a high table or a stand. When it is on the floor, you can group your students around you in the whole group instructional space and look right into their eyes as they cluster around you. At the intermediate level, many teachers find that they are more comfortable placing the overhead projector on a low desk and sitting next to it on a primary child's chair—closer to the floor than if the projector were on a four-foot cart, but not all the way down on the floor. If you leave the overhead projector on a cart and teach while all of your students sit at their desks, you risk reducing the intimacy of the experience. Writing is hard to do, and as teachers, we have the responsibility of showing our students that we struggle with the process, too. Writing in front of our students, just as we ask them to do on their own, privileges them with seeing the process in action, rather than simply having it assigned to them. It is also beneficial for us since engaging in the act of writing ourselves reminds us that writing is no simple task, and we develop more respect for what we are asking our students to do. The best teachers of writing are those who actually write themselves!

Do Students Have a Sense of How the Environment Has Been Organized?

> *Children should be able to take guests through their classroom on a tour, identifying different areas and materials and their purposes. Joanne Hindley shares a personal discovery related to such a task.*
>
> I realized this was something I needed to think more about when a group of teachers visited my own classroom. I asked a few students to take them on a "walking tour" of our room and point out anything they felt the visitors should know about. Later, in discussing the morning visit, the teachers commented on how well the students seemed to know their space. But as they listed the different areas of the room the children had pointed out, I was more struck by what the children left out than by what they included. They never mentioned numerous bulletin boards, and the teachers noted that they skimmed right over whole sections of the room. These, I realized, were the areas the children never interacted with. (Hindley 1996, 6)

If students are unable to articulate the reasons for the objects and structures that are in the classroom setting, teachers must consider their value. If children are blind to their environment and do not understand what the items on the walls are for or how the classroom library is organized, for example, it is probably time to take a step back and review or re-introduce those areas. It may end up that there are some elements that can be removed, clearing up more time or space for valuable instructional activities.

Efficiency and Effectiveness Task

Student-Led Classroom Tours

Invite your students to give a tour of your classroom to one of your colleagues. After the tour, sit down and discuss what the students pointed out and what they left out. Return to the room arrangement task you completed earlier in this chapter. What physical parts of the room need to be changed? What is on the walls that needs to be addressed with students or redone? Note on your room arrangement chart which changes you would like to make immediately and which you will implement the following school year.

How Does the Classroom Sound?

Organizing for space in the classroom is more than simply what goes into it. You also need to take a closer look at what goes on within it. As the old saying goes: It is not what you have, it is how you use it.

Within a well-managed classroom, there will be noise. Caine and Caine (1994) include in their twelve principles of brain-based learning that the human brain is a social brain and that people need to talk as they learn and process new information. Learners solidify concepts as they reflect on them orally and work to understand new learning together. Teachers must honor this by not only giving students permission and time to talk but by teaching them how to do so in a productive manner. Productive talk is not yelling and hollering; nor is it talking in a respectable tone on a subject completely unrelated to the task at hand.

> Teachers often report that when they begin using groups, they are bothered by the increased noise level. A common guideline is the use of the "six-inch" or "twelve-inch" voice. Another is to speak quietly enough so that students in nearby groups can't hear or aren't distracted. "Whisper voices" does not work well as a guideline, because groups usually can't work efficiently and conduct conversations while whispering. (Everston, Emmer, and Worsham 2003, 116)

Whose Voices Do I Hear? What Are They Saying?

If a classroom resonates constantly with the teacher's voice, something is wrong. A necessary component of learning is talking. When children talk over newly acquired information, their brains are able to weigh that information against existing knowledge and file it away in an appropriate and logical location for later retrieval (Caine and Caine 1994). However, there is such a thing as too much student talk. Classrooms can be somewhat noisy places, but they should not be consistently characterized as such. The nature of the noise is what is important. What are the students talking about? Are students and teachers talking to each other or at each other? Are the volume and tone respectful?

Are the Students and Teachers Aware of Their Own Voices?

This refers not only to what is said, but how it is said. Oftentimes, in classrooms, students and teachers battle to be heard, each getting progressively louder in order to be heard over the other. Instead of raising your voice in order to get your students' attention, try lowering your voice, getting quieter and quieter so they have to strain to hear you. Teachers do not need to yell or raise their voices in the classroom. If this is a characteristic of yourself and you find your throat raw and your voice hoarse at the end of every day, you need to consider why this is so. Consider, too, the tone that you use with your students. We all get frustrated at times, but yelling at students or using a demeaning or degrading tone is not a successful way in which to get quiet, attention, or respect. Think of yourself and how you react when someone responds or reacts to you in an inappropriate volume or tone. Such inappropriateness is usually indicative of underlying management problems that have not been addressed. The desire to yell or scold is a symptom of a problem that can be dealt with using the ideas and suggestions found throughout this text.

Remember that all of your actions are models and demonstrations for your students. Their behavior will mimic yours, to a degree, and as a community, you all need to learn how to use the volume and tone of your voice effectively. Our voices are powerful management tools: We can either escalate or diffuse situations, depending on how we use them.

How Effectively Can the Teacher Get Students' Attention?

In a busy classroom, a teacher needs to be able to get the attention of all the students in the classroom. This should happen quickly and without the teacher having to raise his or her voice inappropriately. Refer to Chapter 2 for more information on effective strategies for getting students' attention quickly.

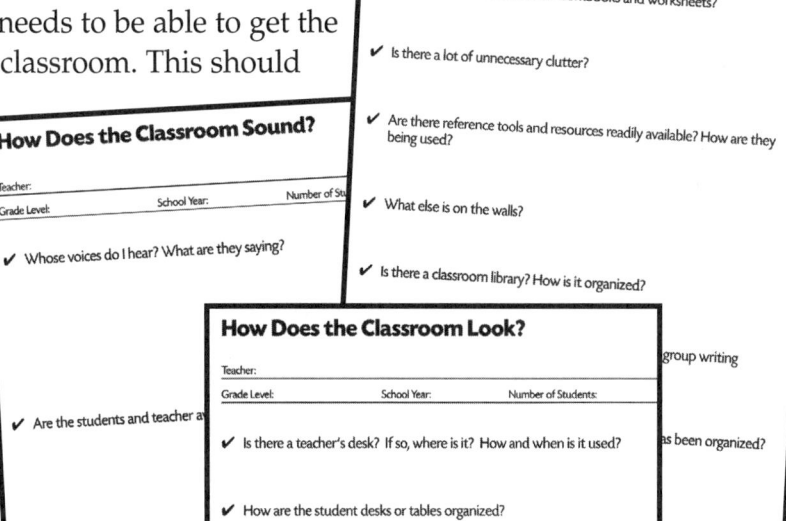

Efficiency and Effectiveness Task

Reanalyzing Your Classroom Environment

Revisit the checklists you completed earlier in this chapter on "How Does the Classroom Feel?" "How Does the Classroom Look?" and "How Does the Classroom Sound?" Make notes next to the items that you would like to change, modify, or implement after reading through this chapter.

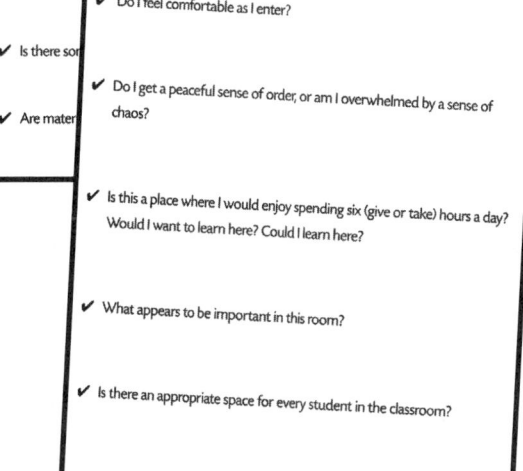

Chapter 2

Organizing for Time

Intermediate teachers sometimes overwhelm themselves with their responsibility to cover a large amount of material in a limited amount of time. It is at this point that teachers need to stop and take time to reflect. Refer to the two questions introduced in the Introduction:

- **Why am I doing this?**
- **How is it good for children?**

When teachers focus on the previous questions, they may find that much of the pressure they are feeling has been self-imposed and unnecessary.

Fountas and Pinnell remind us that, as teachers, "there are more demands on your time than you can accommodate" and that "every moment you save by establishing routines, you will realize in instruction" (Fountas and Pinnell 2001, 100). What this chapter on organizing for time boils down to is helping you as a teacher to figure out what you do every day, and then finding a way to make it faster and easier—efficiency and effectiveness at their best!

Finding Time to Fit It All In

As teachers implement effective teaching practices, their major concern is often the time factor. Many have been heard citing the following: "How on earth can we do all of this? We have so many content area responsibilities, there is no way we can cover all of our curriculum *and* do all of this literacy stuff!"

Get to know your students, your curriculum, and your materials. Add to that a solid theory to base your instruction on, and time will find you. Always ask: Why am I doing this? How is it good for children?

As I worked with a group of teachers who were struggling to find time to implement the new literacy practices their district was mandating, they gave me an example of a dinosaur unit they needed to teach for science. They explained in great detail all of the things that they incorporated into this extensive study that left them no time to engage in literacy instruction. Equally overwhelmed by the daunting task they were burdened with, I had to agree with them. How on earth would there be time for literacy instruction with all of these content area requirements? In an effort to help them resolve this problem, I asked for the curriculum guide. I found the section that referred to dinosaurs: Children will know and understand that dinosaurs are extinct. One sentence. That was it! I imagine the unit they created is loads of fun, and I am sure the children learn a great deal about dinosaurs—but at what cost? —Lisa

Chapter 2: Organizing for Time

> *I had only been teaching for four years when I was first stricken with what I call the "filing cabinet flu." It was toward the end of September and time to dig into my files in search of the folders dedicated to my next unit of instruction. As I dug through the folders, examples of theme-related artwork, worksheets, writing frames, projects, poems, and all other manner of things began to pile up on the tables, chairs, and floor space surrounding my cabinet. Every file I pulled out provided yet another related activity from my undergraduate idea portfolio, my teaching days in numerous classrooms and grade levels, district sharing sessions, countless workshops, and teacher magazines full of activities, writing prompts, and art projects. At last the pile stopped growing and I was able to begin my planning. I imagine you can relate to the dismay I experienced when I finally managed to sort through all of the activities and found that to fit them all in, I should have begun my unit two weeks earlier in order for it to have been completed six weeks later, at the end of October! Fortunately, I stopped and asked myself: Why am I doing this? How is it good for children? As I considered these two questions, I narrowed down my selections to include only those activities that served a true purpose (not just a "fun" activity), and I reduced this six-week investigation to a more reasonable amount of time—two weeks. It was a good thing I did as most of my answers to the first question were "Because it matches my theme," "Because it is fun," or "Because the students (or their parents) will like it." I found few answers to the second question.* —Lisa

Ultimately, you need to find and keep activities that are of the most value in developing students' academic and social-emotional skills, knowledge, and habits. "In thinking about my beliefs I realize that not every curriculum area can receive equal attention. The only thing we accomplish by spreading ourselves too thin is to set ourselves up to feel mediocre, and teaching deserves much more than mediocrity" (Hindley 1996, xix). It is a good idea to plan most of your instruction before you open your filing cabinet. This way, you reflect on your curriculum and the needs of your students first and the contents of the filing cabinet second. If an activity is truly worthwhile, you will remember it when the next year rolls around; however, always check the files, just in case you have forgotten something that would provide a brilliant teaching opportunity. And don't forget—one of the easiest and most effective ways of streamlining instruction and finding more time in your day is through integrating your instruction within and across the content areas.

Section 1

Scheduling: Putting the Puzzle Pieces Together

Think about organizing your daily schedule as a puzzle that can be put together in a variety of ways. Start out with a list of all the pieces you know you need to include, whether it is during single blocks or periods, or across the entire day, depending upon how your school has chosen to organize its intermediate grades. After constructing this list, consider the structures that you cannot control, such as specials, and then start to put together the puzzle. The Efficiency and Effectiveness Task will be helpful as you work through this list to organize your personal puzzle pieces into something unique that works for you.

▶ Efficiency and Effectiveness Task

Make a "Clean Sweep"

There is a reality show on The Learning Channel (TLC) called *Clean Sweep*. Each episode begins with a team working with a family to sort their household belongings and possessions into categories. On the show, three piles are constructed out on the front lawn labeled something to the effect of: "Things to Keep," "Things to Toss," and "Things to Donate." We suggest doing the same for your classroom in order to make a "clean sweep" of your instructional arena.

1. **Write a list of all the things you do throughout your school day that take time.** Include everything that you can think of, but be as specific as possible. Do not forget recess, bathroom breaks, and morning announcements. Also, break down blocks of instruction, making them as clear as possible. For example, with literacy, list spelling, vocabulary, read alouds, daily writing mini-lesson, etc. If it takes time out of your day, it needs to be recorded, and done so in as narrow a fashion as possible so that you can start the process of arranging, changing, and/or releasing your puzzle pieces.

2. **Engage in what is typically used as a content area instructional activity called List-Group-Label activity** (Tierney, Readence, and Dishner, 1990). Take the entire list and start to organize it into categories. Feel free to use an "open sort" process wherein you create your own categories based on what you see, or use a "closed sort" based on the following categories: "NO FLEXIBILITY" (areas you have no control over, such as when recess, lunch, or specials occur); "SOME FLEXIBILITY" (this may include some school-required activities such as attendance taking, or instructional areas such as social studies or science that you may not have to teach every day, or in isolation); and "GREAT FLEXIBILITY" (this category might include things like collecting homework or bathroom routines). You should also create a "Things to Toss" category, consisting of unnecessary, time-intensive activities.

3. **Now begin the process of determining where you can find or create more time throughout your day by examining each of the items in each category.** As you create your puzzle, begin with the foundational pieces that are inflexible and then work from there. A true "clean sweep" of your classroom!

An interesting and enlightening twist on this process would be to ask your students to do the activity as well. You might be amazed at the things that appear on their lists that do not have a presence on yours. Their sorting process can be an open or closed one and will provide you with great insight into how your classroom is really operating.

Chapter 2: Organizing for Time

> During the writing of this book, I shared an experience that nearly drove me from the classroom. I had only been teaching for five years, but already, I was at the end of my rope. Somehow, I had become one of those teachers that the principal seemed to count on for everything: Primary Team Leader, chair of school improvement team, mentor to five new teachers, student teacher supervisor, assessment coordinator, disciplinarian to many students from other classes, and an after-school teacher. And those responsibilities were in addition to the standard teacher duties which included my own class of 30 students, lunch duty, recess duty, etc. Sound familiar?
>
> It was flattering to be trusted with such important responsibilities, but I was overwhelmed and exhausted. My professional life and personal life both began to suffer. In order to "save myself," I decided to tender my resignation. Fortunately, I was working with a set of colleagues and a principal who recognized that my feelings were not a result of my inability to succeed in any of these tasks. The problem was that I was trying to succeed in all of these tasks.
>
> I learned a powerful lesson that year: Quality is better than quantity. We can only do so much as teachers, and one of the most important things that we can learn to do is to say "No!" when our plate starts to get full. A happy and healthy life outside of the classroom will lead to a more productive life within the classroom!
>
> What I learned from my experiences is that not only is it important to organize for time during the school day when I am, in the words of Joanne Hindley, "in the company of children," I must also consider how I am using my time outside of the classroom. Taking on too many responsibilities or organizing lesson planning and student assessment efforts inefficiently outside of the classroom incurs great stress and leaves little to no time for other equally important things in the lives of a teacher: friends, family, and time to do the things we need and love to do! —Sarah

As you are the only one who knows the specifics of your school day, the building of your puzzle is up to you. The daily puzzle pieces for teachers to keep in mind as they structure their day vary depending on the grade level, time of year, and the attention span of students. Some days, you might spend a bit more time in one area and a bit less in another, but remember, your goal is to figure out what you do every day, and then figure out a way to make it faster, easier, and more productive.

To fit everything in, teachers need to create an orderly environment with minimal disruption and wasted time, allowing students to concentrate on their learning (Everston, Emmer, and Worsham 2003, 20). To achieve this orderly environment, plan procedures carefully and look closely at the decisions you make as you build your day, returning again to the two questions that guide classroom decisions: Why am I doing this? How is it good for children?

There are many ways that teachers can work to recover lost or hidden time in their daily schedule. Do you have double specials every day? Could you creatively combine some things, such as incorporating independent reading time into your independent work time? Additional daily independent reading could even occur during the transition into your daily closing. As students wrap up their work, they could sit on the floor with the book they are taking home that day and read.

Another way to find additional instructional time is to write daily schedules for your classroom. Look for the simple tasks that you can get out of the way quickly and easily, or dole out some of those responsibilities to others. Taking attendance or collecting field trip forms does not have to be a lengthy process. You can have students leave money and forms in a basket to be checked later. Taking attendance can be as simple as taking a look around and identifying empty seats or having children move a card with their name or picture on it from one side of a board to the other, indicating their presence. Fitting it all in is a distinct possibility, as long as you are conscious about how you spend every minute of your day.

Efficiency and Effectiveness Task

Finding Lost Time

Consider working as a private detective within your own classroom and search for those lost instructional minutes and seconds within your day. To begin, fill out the schedules for an upcoming week (see the appendix for full blackline masters). As you read through the strategies in this section, note where you can make changes or rearrange your priorities to reclaim instructional time.

Creating More Minutes in the Day

A study of 105 primary students by Leinhardt, Zigmond, and Cooley (1981) notes that well over an hour each day was spent in waiting, transitions, management, and other activities..." (Allington 2001, 31). Just think of what you could do if you corralled all those wasted minutes and seconds—in total, you would add almost twenty-eight days to the school year!

An orderly, cooperative classroom does not happen overnight. It is a product of demonstration, explicit teaching, and practice" (Fountas and Pinnell 2001, 97). Appropriate modeling, direct instruction, and practice of certain routines and behaviors may not always be effective, though, so if a routine or practice is not working for you and your students, change it. It is not sufficient that it worked for Sarah and Lisa, your friend down the hall, or a speaker whose session you attended. We are all unique teachers with radically differing classrooms, and what works in one classroom may not work in another.

The following are some suggestions to consider and choose from that will allow you to recapture lost time, creating more minutes in your day.

> It is only when students negotiate acceptable behaviors and routines with the teacher and assume responsibility for putting them into practice that we can effectively teach...When students have a say in how the classroom is organized and managed, they take more responsibility for putting rules and routines into practice. All of us work harder to achieve a goal when we have been part of the decision making process that has gone into attaining it, as opposed to being told what to do. (Routman 2000, 539–540)

Classroom Entry Routines

Efficiently and effectively run classrooms begin functioning as such the very second children enter the classroom. There is no "dead" or "lost" time whatsoever. It is a good practice to have a consistent entry routine for children to follow that will allow for the students and the teacher to go about their business of settling in in a predictable manner. Establish a logical routine for this that is an easy and productive one for both the students and the teacher. For example, consider beginning each day with journal writing, independent reading, or with an open-ended math inquiry to be worked through (i.e., How many different ways can you construct a problem whose answer is 57?). In each of these cases, all students are able to work almost indefinitely on a task that is easily geared to varied levels.

Such routines need to be clearly established and the parameters for each clearly defined. Be watchful, though. The routine needs to be taught, modeled, and practiced—consider the gradual release of responsibility model—in order for it to work. If a routine is not going well, look first to the teaching that preceded it. Was it introduced properly? Explained and modeled and practiced thoroughly? If not, the fault lies with the teacher, not with the students, and the teacher has the responsibility for providing the necessary support in order for the system to be a productive one. At times, routines are simply "not right" for a variety of reasons, and another one needs to be selected and properly introduced. Don't automatically assume that what worked last year, or what works for the teacher across the hall, will work *this* year, in *your* classroom.

There are certain "morning routines" that seem to be standard in most intermediate classrooms: taking attendance, turning in homework, and collecting lunch money (or field trip money, book fair money, etc.). Each of these routines falls into the category of things that need to be done, but that are characterized with some degree of flexibility. It is rarely required that such tasks be done the very second that students enter the classroom, or that they are performed by the teacher. There are infinite ways in which teachers and students can work together to ensure that these tasks are accomplished accurately and in a timely fashion.

Section 1

Taking Attendance

For example, attendance does not have to be taken as the teacher reads off every name, waiting for confirmation by each individual student with a "Good morning!", "Here!", or "Present!" Consider how much time this takes and then multiply that by 180 or more if you teach multiple groups of students throughout the day. Easier ways of taking attendance that will give time back to you and your students include such approaches as the following:

- Establish the entry routine as one that requires students to be in their seats working. Wait until the proper time and, as students are engaged in their routine morning task, you can take attendance at a glance by noting who is *not* present, rather than by who *is*.

- Organize a system using cards or magnets that students can move from one location to another, indicating their presence in the classroom. In order to ensure that no cards have been moved incorrectly, a quick head count can be done to check the number of students who are present against the data presented through the check-in system. This system is similar to those used in many workplaces; when you arrive, you subtly but explicitly make your presence known.

- Have a student take responsibility for taking attendance. You may choose to have a partner or yourself confirm the record.

- Depending upon your school's policy, you may be able to take attendance later in the morning when the classroom entry "rush hour" has ended.

Turning in Homework

In many classrooms, collecting homework becomes a chore that lasts longer than it actually took students to complete their homework! In others, it may not take a great deal of time on a daily basis, but when you add up the minute or two it takes to do it for each period and then multiply that across the year, you will find that an amazing amount of time is invested in a task that can be accomplished far more quickly. Consider simply having a basket available in the classroom (not right at the door as it will cause a classroom entry traffic jam in the hallway) for students to deposit their work in as soon as their backpacks have been put away, but before they settle into the morning routine.

Chapter 2: Organizing for Time

If you are concerned about knowing which students did or did not complete and turn in their homework right away, consider this idea that Sarah's third grade teammate found to be useful:

At the beginning of the year, each of my students was assigned a number from 1–26 that became his or her identifying tag throughout the school year. In the upper right corner of all of their papers, the students would record their assigned number. Every day after homework was turned in to the "Homework" basket, a student helper would take the stack of papers and place them in numerical order. Either the student or I could take a quick look at the papers, easily identifying what, if any, numbers were missing in the sequence. —Lisa Bernstein; Third Grade Teacher; Evanston, Illinois

Collecting Money

Most teachers collect money from their students either on a regular basis for lunch or other fees, or on an irregular basis for such things as field trips, book orders, or other special events and activities. There is a certain urgency to this routine as it has to do with finances that are best in the hands of the teacher, given busy and crowded classrooms. For that reason, the collection of money needs to be done in an expedient manner, and is often best left to the teacher, depending on the particular classroom. Collecting lunch money may be something that can be discussed and negotiated at school or grade level meetings. Does it need to be collected right away? Every day? Are there different ways of doing this that make more sense? This routine may be one that the teacher decides to take greater responsibility for due to the sensitive nature of financial business, especially given the varied lunch rates of different students in the classroom that need not be made public knowledge. Lunch count can easily be taken in similar ways to the morning attendance, or left up to a student leader each day, but the money needs to be handled by the teacher. Work with your school staff or grade level team to come up with a different routine or policy if collecting lunch money is something that you feel takes up considerable amounts of instructional time.

When it comes to other types of money to be collected, it may be wisest, in an effort to rescue precious school day minutes, not to count students' money immediately as it comes in. Book order or field trip money should be turned in in a sealed envelope or resealable bag, with the student's name on or inside it. Have additional envelopes or resealable bags readily available in a designated location for students who come to school with fists of change. Collect this money and hold it in a secure location, but wait until later in the day to actually sort through it. This may be done during a lunch break or prep or after school, but the minimal sacrifice of time here will be a healthy trade-off for the instructional time you reclaim. Parent helpers can also assist with collecting money.

Section 1

After several months of growing frustration over the rampant misbehavior of students in our school, the staff was determined to discover the source and rid ourselves of this problem that was negatively impacting the entire school community, both inside and outside of the classrooms. We decided that we would tackle the problem by identifying the areas of greatest concern and begin working from there. The entire staff began to meticulously record the time, location, and nature of student misbehavior, and we quickly discovered a trend. The majority of the problems we were dealing with on a regular basis had their origins in the "un-manned" hallways before and after school, and during transition times.

It had never occurred to us, but we discovered that every one of us had chosen these few small windows of time—just before and after school and in between periods or classes—to scurry around in our classroom making last-minute preparations. The scurrying allowed for us to be prepared when students finally entered the classroom, but the complete absence of hallway leadership and support for learning proper hallway behavior had resulted in the unorganized chaos that was the perfect breeding ground for the misbehavior that characterized these pockets of time.

After coming to this realization, the entire staff agreed that each and every classroom teacher, "specials" teacher, custodian, cafeteria worker, and the principal would work together to solve this problem by sacrificing the few extra planning minutes the transition times offered, and placing ourselves instead in the hallways to guide the students' behavior so that it was more conducive to smooth transitions.

In order to develop appropriate independent hallway behavior, we worked to create a positive tone, learning as many students' names as possible, and by addressing them personally. We worked individually and as a staff to establish appropriate hallway routines and behaviors the same way that we worked to do so within our classrooms, and the benefits of our efforts were soon realized. The hallways became a more peaceful place that complemented the learning going on within classrooms, rather than competing or interfering with it. —Sarah

Chapter 2: Organizing for Time

> ### Efficiency and Effectiveness Task
>
> **Solving Problems**
>
> *Being proactive as suggested in the Preface is a healthy way to ensure minimal management problems to a degree, but it is not fail-safe. There will be problems in all classrooms and all schools that teachers must work to understand in order to solve them.*
>
> In order to solve problems in school-wide management and student behavior, it is important to be as acutely aware of the problem as possible. Follow the model used by Sarah's school in the preceding story about solving student misbehavior in order to determine where to dedicate your time and energy in developing a more productive learning environment.
>
> 1. Work over a 1–2 week period as an entire staff to create a data log of when and where problems occur outside of the classroom, and the details related to those problems. It may be valuable to indicate who was involved, and which of the problems were more severe.
>
> 2. After collecting individual and office data over this time period, regroup as a staff and analyze your findings. Are there detectable patterns?
>
> 3. Determine which of the pattern sets you would like to address as a whole staff and then create a plan together.
>
> 4. Implement your plan.
>
> 5. After a designated period of time, evaluate the results. Be sure to include how the staff did in your evaluation, not just the students.
>
> Keep in mind, it is important that this entire process is done by the entire staff, not a small committee or the principal alone. This process can also be extremely valuable when used at the individual classroom level.

Transitions

Children like and thrive on predictable sequences of events in their day (Forester and Reinhard 1994); therefore, it is important to ensure that there are clear routines, including transitions, for students to follow. It is wise to devise a quick attention-getting device. Many teachers ring a bell or use a rain stick or chimes, some dim the lights, and some raise their hand and wait for others to follow. Chose a device that is age appropriate, comfortable, and that works for both you and your students and institute it. Whatever system you choose, take the following precautions:

- **If you use a clap system, do not attempt to use it to double as a mathematics activity by changing the pattern every time you do it.** This will not command immediate attention. (Think how ridiculous it would be if the principal changed the fire alarm every time there was a fire or a drill.)

- **Be sure to teach children from day one to freeze and attend to you and only you immediately on recognizing the signal.** If you are not insistent on this from the start, children will not learn to respond appropriately.

- **Be prepared to give immediate, precise, and concise directions within seconds after getting attention.** If you are talking to only one or a few children or dawdle or drone, your students will learn very quickly that your message is unimportant and will continue the activity they were engaged in instead of listening to you.

- **Give your students an appropriate "Heads up!" prior to major transitions.** It is unfair of us as teachers to expect children to immediately stop and switch activities on command without privileging them with a prior warning. It is respectful for us to let them know that a transition will be occurring in 1–2 minutes (or whatever time frame makes sense given the current activity) so that they can begin to prepare mentally and/or physically. This can also serve as a helpful tool for children who consistently need more time than others. If that warning is provided, certain children can begin to transition at that moment, ensuring that all students will be ready to fully transition at the proper time.

- **If the system you choose is not working, change it!**

Bathroom Routines

Do you bring your entire class to the restroom at the same time? How many times a day? How long does it take? Now, you do the math. How much time are you losing? Consider teaching children how to be responsible for going to the bathroom on their own. This would include instruction on the most direct route and how to behave in the hallway, use the restroom, wash hands, leave the bathroom ready for the next person, and return to class promptly. Easy, independent bathrooms routines include:

- Post a "sign out" sheet at the door. If a student needs to use the bathroom, the student simply writes down his or her name and goes. Upon returning, her or she crosses out the name.

- Similarly, but more environmentally conscious, have a set of clothespins or markers of some sort with students' names on them by the door. If a student needs to use the restroom, the marker is moved to a card that says "Restroom" and is returned when the student returns to the classroom.

> *Rather than constructing an elaborate bathroom routine, I simply made a small wooden bathroom pass that was left next to the classroom door. When a student needed to use the restroom, he or she would simply take the pass, place it on his or her desk, and leave the room and return quickly, quietly, and unobtrusively. Children knew they were not allowed to do this during whole group instructional time, only during independent or small work time. No one missed whole group lessons, and I could tell at a glance who was gone! —Sarah*

If it is impossible for you to organize an independent bathroom procedure, find a way to make use of this time so that it is not lost. Bring along a read aloud or a book of math riddles or mental math teasers, or make it part of recess.

"I'm waiting... I'm waiting..."

If you find yourself standing arms crossed, tapping your foot, repeating this like a broken record or even docking recess time as a trade-off, ask yourself why it is that your students are making you wait. What is it that you are doing next that they are uninterested in? Have you given them the message that promptness is not important and that you will wait for them? If you call students to the floor and then spend five minutes getting ready while they sit there, they will learn quickly that their time is much better spent if they ignore you at first, then show up five minutes later when you are actually prepared.

Students will transition promptly when teachers are fully prepared to move through the lessons of the day. Try not to ask your students to move unless you are ready to proceed with your next lesson. If your classroom is organized and free of clutter, the materials you need will be readily available. If you have worked to streamline your day, you will find that your students will respond appropriately to your call for attention or movement. They will learn quickly that the activities that fill their days are all authentic and engaging activities that serve a purpose. It is very difficult to maintain the attention of students if you lose the momentum and smoothness in the day. Effective teachers are well prepared and maintain an appropriate pace and focus in their lessons. Moving too slowly or quickly, going on tangents, and giving in to distractions will only lead to less productive teaching and learning.

Lining Up

Does it take forever before you can leave your classroom? Try switching tasks around in your schedule. For example, end your lesson a minute or two early, and take that time to play mental math games or sing a song. While the class is engaged in this activity, they can also be putting away textbooks, folders, papers, or whatever it is that often takes five or more extra minutes to take care of before they get into line.

Remember that waiting in line is not an exciting activity that encourages promptness—unless students are vying for a place at the front of the line, which may result in an even larger problem. What can you do to encourage promptness and minimize wasted time? You might consider using standing-in-line time to play daily games with your word wall. For example, "I'm thinking of a term that tells how someone can move," or use the time for content area games such as Scattegories® ("I am thinking of animals that are herbivores").

Recess

Children need to play, but take care with how much time is being devoted to this activity. Also, think about when you schedule this time.

Do you teach a full day and have trouble getting your students back in from the playground? You might want to try flip-flopping lunch and recess. It might be preferable for students to miss a few minutes of lunchtime than mathematics time.

> *When working to include recess in our busy day, I had to balance the necessity of play and the amount of transitional time it took us to get dressed and undressed before and after going outside. My solution? I moved recess from the middle of my day to the end. My children got ready to go home and dressed twice as quickly as they were motivated to play (as opposed to standing in line, bored or misbehaving while waiting for their bus) and I rescued valuable instructional time on both sides of a mid-day recess. —Lisa*

If switching around your schedule is not an option, you may want to consider organizing your schedule so that you have students engaged in an enticing activity after lunch or recess. You can reduce transition time dramatically if students start working on independent activities immediately after lunch or recess (as opposed to waiting for them, and then launching into a whole group lesson once they are all ready).

Jobs

The lyrics of the classic Beatles' (1967) tune "I Get by with a Little Help from My Friends" can help here. It is much easier to accomplish nearly anything with a little extra help, and that is one of the purposes of classroom jobs. If the classroom truly belongs to the entire community it holds, then all of its members should take an active part in maintaining the dynamic and successful functioning of the system. Holding a classroom job also assists children in developing responsible behavior.

To boost student self-esteem (and make tracking jobs easier for you), consider designating one child as the Classroom Assistant for yourself and the room for that day. Students can take turns doing anything and everything that needs to be done that day. Another variation would be to identify a "Table Manager" for each table or cluster of desks. The Table Manager is responsible for making sure that all students are on task and that all student jobs at that table are completed.

There are as many systems for handling jobs and student responsibilities in the classroom as there are classrooms and teachers. The best system is the one that works for you, and it will be different for every teacher!

Chapter 2: Organizing for Time

> *Students need jobs in a classroom to help teach responsibility and to build a sense of community. I never had success keeping track of classroom jobs to make sure they were rotated fairly. Instead I devised a system whereby all my students held jobs for the week. These jobs rotated every Monday, and students looked forward to that change. I created up to 30 jobs (based on my class enrollment) and recorded these individually on 3 x 10 strips of tagboard. These were laminated and then hung vertically from the chalkboard ledge. Each student had a wooden clothespin with his/her name written in permanent marker. Students clipped the clothespins to the job cards to indicate their responsibilities for the week.*
>
> *On Mondays, students randomly drew a number from a basket. The student with #1 chose a job first, followed by student #2, etc. Student #30 took the last job posted. This became a very good opportunity for improving listening skills because students were highly motivated to get a "good" job. I called numbers quickly to be efficient with time. Students not listening who missed their number had to wait to choose a job at the very end. Examples of classroom jobs were line leader, messenger, lunch count taker, pencil sharpener, mail carrier, attendance taker, and agenda keeper. The randomness of assigning jobs was always entertaining. Some students were lucky and pulled "low" numbers each week, giving them a chance to get the more popular jobs. Leaving this up to chance was always more easily accepted by my students than if I assigned jobs.* —Amy Goodman; Middle School Literacy Teacher; Anchorage, Alaska

Snack

If your intermediate students have a snack during the day, you may want to consider designating a time for snack and asking your students to bring their own. Snack time is important as students need to fuel their systems on a regular basis, and it also provides an opportunity for them to develop their social and interactive skills as they chat away while they eat.

There are ways to honor both of these needs while not sacrificing valuable instructional and learning time. During snack time, allow students to continue working on whatever independent or small group task they are engaged in while they munch on their snack. Help your students learn that there is no snack "time"; instead, the time they eat their snack runs concurrently with other activities. A student can be snuggled up in the book corner reading while munching away, as another student works in the writing center, pausing every now and then for a nibble. Other students may be working jointly on a task, working, eating, and conversing at the same time.

It is important to teach appropriate routines, and it is well worth the time spent in the long run. For example, make sure students are aware of how sticky fingers can dirty or damage books or computers. This provides an excellent opportunity for a class discussion—students can identify the problem and test out possible solutions. It is also in your best interest to teach your students how to clean up after themselves. They need to be aware of crumbs on the floor and spills on tables and act responsibly by taking care of their mess using paper towels or sponges that are always available to them. If you are worried that some children will forget their snack, organize an "Extra Snack" basket that children can donate to. If they bring a snack they do not like, they can trade. If someone forgets, they can grab one and then bring an extra the next day.

The following are some additional helpful hints for snack time:

- You might discourage bringing in drinks. Human bodies are made up of over 80 percent water, and the source that comes straight out of the drinking fountain serves as one of the best "brain foods" around. Students should have constant access to water, whether it is through unlimited access to the drinking fountain or a water bottle kept on their desks. If you observe students abusing drinking fountain privileges, do not take them away. Ask yourself, "Why? Are they really that thirsty or are they avoiding some other task?" Direct your energy to the source of the problem, not toward the symptom.

- Use this time to encourage good eating habits that will last a lifetime. Teach students to bring in healthy foods. Foods without labels (e.g., fruits and vegetables) are the best, but take some time looking at those that do have labels. If you and your students cannot pronounce the words, you might want to help them reconsider using it as fuel for their bodies.

Having a Backup Plan

It is important to always have a backup plan that students can easily and automatically refer to, either when they have completed a task early or when you are pulled away from instruction momentarily. The easiest thing to do is to teach your students to have something to read and something to write on immediately available to them. Personal or group book boxes on each table are a must. Include a variety of texts that are both interesting and accessible in these boxes. Add small versions of big books, texts that children have used in small reading groups, student-written and published texts, and copies of old favorites. If you are a specials teacher, or are teaching in a specific content area, you can choose a similar activity more relevant to that academic area. See the suggestions in Chapter 7 for further ideas.

> Periodically, you will have to fill in time between activities or before and after major transitions... Filling these times with a constructive activity is better than trying to stretch out an already completed task or just letting students amuse themselves... accumulate a file so you will be ready with a filler when one is needed. (Everston, Emmer, and Worsham 2003, 67)

Organizing and Passing Out Materials

"The more students can do independently and the quicker they can do it, the more they can go on learning and have time for learning on their own. Make sure students know how to find and access the words, supplies, and books they read" (Routman 2003, 210).

There are some items that every student should have on hand all the time, such as writing utensils, paper, and an independent reading book. Other items may need to be passed out for the time being, and then recollected for future use. Take a close look at which items fall into which categories in your classroom and consider the amount of time that is spent on a regular basis passing out and recollecting items. If your students do not have certain items in their own personal material kits, take the time to figure out whether that is the best decision. Oftentimes, teachers do not allow students to maintain their own materials as they are concerned that students will lose them or do not know how to use them properly. If this is the case in your classroom, a primary and necessary solution is to devote some of your instructional time to teaching your students how to use, respect, care for, and maintain such objects. Students can and will be responsible for their supplies if you teach them how to do so. This may take a considerable amount of time initially, but it will save far more time in the long run.

The same care must be taken in teaching students how to organize their materials so that they are easily accessible and manageable. There are far too many children's desks that are overflowing with old papers, half-eaten snacks, and broken pencils. This is not a sign of an unorganized child; it is a sign of a teacher who has chosen not to help the students in his or her classroom manage their materials in a manner that is conducive to learning.

> *In an effort to save time and enhance instruction, my third-grade teammate and I worked to integrate our instruction across disciplines to the highest degree possible. An example of doing so occurred at the beginning of every school year as we integrated a science unit on "Classification" and the seemingly never-ending task of organizing student desks.*
>
> *We would begin the unit by discussing the reasons for and benefits of classifying. The students would search for different classification systems in their world and would explain how classifying something in a particular way was logical and helpful. To bring the lesson to a higher and more immediately accessible level, we then asked students to consider how what they knew about classification might be helpful in organizing their desks.*
>
> *Students began to suggest and identify logical organizational methods and structures, such as which items should be kept together, which items should be more or less accessible, and why those suggestions made sense. By the end of our discussions, each student had a unique plan for how he or she wanted to organize his or her desk.* —Sarah

Continuing to Teach When Your Students Are No Longer Paying Attention

The attention span of a child in minutes for focused, direct instruction (as opposed to the attention span for playing with a game) is roughly equal to a child's chronological age, translated from years into minutes. For example, a nine year old has an instructional attention span of about nine minutes; a ten year old, ten minutes; and so on. Of course this does not continue on infinitely.

Section 1

> Recent brain research indicates that we have kids' attention for less that ten minutes before they need a "cognitive rest." This means we must allow lots of time for students to process new information, to interact in conversations and collaborative responses. When the work is interesting and we move along at a fast pace, we keep kids engaged. I find that when the lesson is relevant, interesting, and moves along at a good clip, I rarely have to stop and discipline a student. Teaching that keeps kids engaged saves us time and energy. (Routman 2003, 206)

Once anyone is exposed to more than 15–20 minutes of direct instruction wherein the learner is in a fully passive role, attention begins to wander. There are, of course, exceptions. At any level, a truly engaging or active lesson or activity will typically result in an audience that focuses for a longer amount of time. There are variances from child to child, differences depending on the time of day, and from day to day, but take care to monitor the attention of the children in your classroom. You are teaching children, not lessons, and if the children are no longer "with" you, it does not make much sense to continue on with the lesson. Teachers who are attuned to this will find that their planning and teaching becomes almost intuitive.

> Check yourself. How long is it taking you to state your expectations and give directions for independent work? If you can't do this in just a few minutes, the requirements are probably too complicated for students to work without your guidance. Lots of time spent giving directions is time lost from reading instruction and practice. (Routman 2004, 205)

Using the age to minutes ratio will be helpful in providing a rough planning guideline or framework. Design your plans around the windows of optimal learning your group's attention span offers and once you reach that group's limit (or better yet, just before then!), change to an activity that will engage the children actively (Jensen 1995). For example, physically move from the floor to desks, or vice versa; or provide an instructional activity that allows for socializing. If you choose to continue teaching beyond students' attention limits, you run the risk of setting students up for boredom or misbehavior.

A final suggestion for maintaining student attention comes from Regie Routman: "Don't 'stuff' your lessons trying to do everything—it's a sure way to lose kids' attention and interest. Focus on one or two important teaching points, and do them well" (2003, 207).

Efficiency and Effectiveness Task

Planning to Implement Changes

Return to the schedules you completed at the beginning of this chapter. After reading through the strategies and suggestions in this section, review the lists and all the notes you made about rearranging or modifying tasks. How much instructional time do you think you will gain by making modifications to your schedule? In a different color pen, note which changes you would like to implement immediately and which you would like to implement the following school year.

Chapter 3

Organizing for Assessment

> I assess (gather data) and evaluate (analyze that data) as I am teaching. Then I adjust my lesson to meet the needs and interests of my students. I abandon my original plan, I start again, I reteach, I allow more time for discussion, I constantly reflect. This is why all programs have to be modified. We can't just follow the directions of a manual and hope for the best. We don't know what our students will understand or not understand until we begin to work with them. (Routman 2003, 100)

Most researchers agree that assessment should inform instruction (Fountas and Pinnell 1996); therefore, teachers should use assessment to plan for and to evaluate instruction, both in the short and long term. Assessment practices are much more effective when they are woven successfully into the curriculum (Fisher 1991). It is not an efficient use of instructional time to teach children something they already know or to try to bring them to understand something they are not yet ready to learn.

Effective teachers assess their students on an ongoing basis, using both formal and informal assessment tools. "A multidimensional system provides the best chance to collect reliable and valid information on children's progress. The system should include both formal and informal measures; for example, a teacher might combine anecdotal records, lists of books read, running records taken every two or three weeks, a writing sample, and a criterion-referenced standardized test" (Fountas and Pinnell 1996, 76).

Recognizing the importance of assessment for instructional purposes is one thing; managing to organize for it and to incorporate it into an already busy day is another issue altogether.

> *I will never forget the frenzied state the entire teaching staff was reduced to during my introduction to report card time. I, along with my peers, spent days frantically trying to locate, collect, and record last-minute data, and then worked almost around the clock to complete report cards. After dealing with this nightmarish system only once, I had had enough. I was quick to realize that there must be a more purposeful and efficient way of collecting, recording, and storing information, and I have since discovered a number of ways to do so. —Lisa*

Informal Assessment

There are countless opportunities within the school day for effective teachers to engage in informal assessment, collecting information that results in informed instructional decisions. A teacher is wise to seek out these opportunities and capitalize on them. Following are several suggestions for capturing such valuable opportunities.

Anecdotal Records

"Assessment happens all the time, in many contexts—and often when we may least expect it" (Hindley 1996, 136). It is for this very reason that effective teachers must have a well-operating system in place for noting and recording student behaviors that occur outside of formal assessment situations.

No matter how stellar teachers' internal memory devices are, there is no way they can remember all of the important behaviors and displays of learning (academic, social, physical, and behavioral) that students provide on a daily basis. Teachers must first recognize the need for a comfortable system to record such anecdotal observations, and then they must designate time in their schedules to make and record their observations. It is important to have a system in place for both observing and recording (Education Department of South Australia 1991).

Finding a Recording System: Flip Cards, Computer Labels, and Sticky Notes

Three very functional methods of recording observations include using flip cards, computer labels, or sticky notes. It is important to pick a recording system that works best for you.

The flip card method is a simple system for recording and maintaining accurate notes. The system consists of a clipboard and index cards. Label a separate index card with each student's name at the bottom of the card, and then stagger and tape the top edge of the cards onto a clipboard, leaving the names visible. Take notes, adding the date, on the index cards as you make observations. As each card is filled, remove it, file it away, and replace it with a new one. To ensure that you make observations of all your students, it is a

> *I first learned the importance of an accurate and detailed anecdotal record-keeping system as I settled into my first set of parent-teacher conferences and came to a horrible realization: I had nothing concrete to say about many of my students. I found myself making general comments such as "She's a joy to have in class" or "He's progressing quite nicely" or some other equally ambiguous statement, before suggesting to the parents that they hurry on so that they would not be late for their next conference—never mind that our conference still had eighteen minutes left. My comments on students with problems I needed to address were equally pathetic. I would suggest, "She misbehaves constantly" but was completely unable to document any specific instances. Nor could I point out anything the child had done right. At other times, I would generalize "bad" behavior as developmental. I would say, "He'll grow out of it" and pray. —Lisa*

good idea to make a small tally mark next to the child's name every time you make a record.

A variation of the flip card method is to use the same clipboard, only this time, cover it with a sheet of computer labels. At the beginning of the week, write a student's name on each sticker and then take notes on the stickers as you make observations throughout the week. When a sticker is full, you can easily transfer it to the student's folder.

You can also use sticky notes on a clipboard similar to the flip cards and computer labels. Place five to six large sticky notes on a clipboard. Record the name of students you want to observe that day on a sticky note and take notes throughout the day. By observing a different set of students every day, you can collect informal assessment data on every student by the end of the week.

> *In an effort to better organize my anecdotal notes, I used a single computer label for each observation and as I recorded each, I would code the sticker with an "M," "L," "B," or "O" in the upper right corner. Each sticker was then transferred to a different paper in that child's folder: "M" for "Math," "L" for "Literacy," "B" for "Behavior," and "O" for "Other." All of my records were logically organized and easier to access for the purpose of planning assessment and instruction, conferences, and completing report cards. —Sarah*

Scheduling Time to Record Observations

Not only is it important to identify the recording system that will work best for you, it is equally (if not more) important to make sure that you have designated the time you will need to record your observations.

Recording observations regularly will make conferences with parents or staffing meetings a breeze. You will be able to begin a conference identifying specific instances of learning for each child, ensuring the parents or special services team that you know this child well. You can then focus on any areas of concern you have. If your observations are precise and plentiful, the needs of your students will almost always be addressed promptly and with ease.

It is important to schedule a specific time each day to reflect on your assessment routines and take notes on each student.

Section 1

When I first set up a system to take anecdotal notes, I would go days without ever taking a single note. It was about this time that my faithful car took its last breath and forced me to begin my search for a replacement. I found my new car and the solution to my assessment problem at the same time!

Believe it or not, the best thing I ever did to assist in my anecdotal record keeping was to buy an automatic car starter. That's right, an automatic car starter. As I was picking out features for my new car, I fell in love with the automatic car start feature. Just think—I could stand in my apartment, start my car, and let it warm up for five minutes before I even stepped foot outside. A wise purchase for a warm-blooded soul living in Chicago, but one that I could not justify to myself until I made myself a deal.

At the end of every school day, I decided that I would point, aim, and click. My car would start to hum away, while I, living up to the promise I made myself, would sit down and take four or five minutes to jot down anecdotal notes about my students. It was easy to record information about the Student Classroom Assistant—a constant presence during the day. I also found that I could easily make notes about the table group I worked with for writing purposes that day or children from a reading group I met with. As soon as I wrote a comment about one student, I found several more rocketing through my mind. Within weeks, this recording time had become a habit. Long after the snows melted away, I continued to end my day, sitting down at the desk of the Student Classroom Assistant (for perspective) and recording all that I had learned about my students that day. Focusing first on the Student Classroom Assistant ensured me that over a month or so, I would have the opportunity to collect incredible amounts of data on every child in my classroom. —Lisa

Efficiency and Effectiveness Task

Your Own Recording System

To ensure success with anecdotal note taking, identify a recording system you want to use. Then designate specific times to make and record those observations. You may choose to take notes as the last task you do before the end of the day, or you may choose to start your day recording notes from the previous day. Whichever timeframe you choose, make sure it's one you can do every day. If you find that you start off strong but lag off, then try either a different recording system or a different time to take notes. Remember, it is important to find a system that works well for you.

Assessment During Small Reading Groups

Working with small groups of students provides teachers with regular and powerful opportunities to make and record observations on students' literacy development. "While there are many informal reading inventories available as well as all kinds of formal tests, the most accurate information is obtained by carefully observing the child by your side, in the act of reading" (Routman 2003, 100). These notes are invaluable in choosing texts, determining teaching points, and communicating with parents.

Begin every reading group by asking

one child to read the previous session's text as you take a running record while the other children are busy reading other old favorites. Also, make sure to have a "focus child" in every reading group. Take notes on all the children, but take care to have the focus child right next to you so you can make more accurate observations about him or her. The next day, focus on a different child, ensuring that across several sessions, you have had the opportunity to observe each child closely.

Refer to the Small Reading Group Notes (see appendix for full blackline master) for an example of an easy system to implement. Record your general notes for each lesson on the corresponding day, and fill in the lower boxes with students' names and notes you take as you observe your children reading. Keeping these forms on a clipboard (one for each reading group) will allow you to monitor progress throughout the year.

Student Writing Assessments

"In their writing workshops, we advise teachers to teach the writer not the writing. We say, 'If you intervene in such a way that the writing gets better but the writer learns nothing that he can use on another day or another piece, you've gained little. We need to teach the writer strategies that he can use on future days, in future writing'" (Calkins, Montgomery, and Santman 1998, 105). Writing conferences are both an assessment and instructional opportunity teachers engage in on an ongoing basis.

> *Initially, my writing assessment consisted of collecting my students' writing and then marking up their papers, indicating everything that they had done wrong. I would finish off what I considered to be quality assessment by adding on one of many irrelevant comments that I had found in a teacher's book of authentic comments to write on students' papers. "Way to go!" "Good job!" "Nice effort!" Exceptional work received the same comments, only I would add a comma and the child's name before the exclamation point.*
>
> *It was not a very productive use of my time, and I am horrified today to think of how I made those children feel. They did the best they could, and the only response I made was to point out all their errors. In my defense, I thought I was helping them. After all, how else would they learn what to do if I did not tell them? I was afraid that if I did not point out all the errors, that they might have been repeated. —Lisa*

A more beneficial assessment for students is to focus on a child's strengths and to choose a few areas to work on and improve at one time, rather than to try to "fix" everything at once. Two systems that will assist teachers in assessing writing and coordinating productive conferences are Sandwich Cookie Conferences and a simple T-diagram labeled "I'm learning to…" and "I can… ."

Sandwich Cookie Conferences

A sandwich cookie makes a great metaphor for how to make conferencing with students about their writing manageable. Sandwich cookies come in many varieties but only two sizes: regular or double stuffed. If you attempt to make the sandwich cookie too large by adding more filling, it falls apart—the same is true of writing conferences.

Begin every conference with a "cookie wafer." Direct the child's attention to something specific in his or her writing that he or she has done well. This will start the conference on a good note and reinforce a positive aspect of the child's writing. Add "cream filling" in the form of one or two teaching points (remember, sandwich cookies only come in regular or double stuffed). Make the teaching point(s), related to content or mechanics, very focused and specific, highlighting elements of that child's writing that he or she needs to direct attention to. If you try to add more "cream filling" by covering too many teaching points, the conference will fall apart and the child will gain little or nothing from it. Close the conference with another "cookie wafer" or something else that child did well. Again, be very specific so that the child is aware of that strength and will continue to incorporate it into his or her writing.

I'm Learning To.../I Can... T-Diagram

Another way to assess student writing is to document the teaching points addressed in a writing conference, using a simple T-diagram. On the left-hand side of the diagram, record "I am learning to..." and on the right-hand side record "I can...." You can then glue or staple this document into the inside front cover of students' writing journals, notebooks, or folders.

As you conference with a child, refer to the T-diagram as you address different teaching points. As you identify something for that child to work on, jot it down in simple terms in the "I'm learning to..." column, along with the date. Refer to the "I'm learning to..." column at your next conference with that child and use that, in part, to guide your conversation. If the child has demonstrated over several pieces of writing that he or she has mastered that skill, celebrate that fact, and record it in the "I can..." column.

With intermediate students, these forms are valuable tools that can be used as customized, personalized editing checklists for individual students as they write independently or prepare for conferences. They are also valuable resources that can be used for peer-editing purposes, supporting students as they develop their peer-editing skills. (See the appendix for a full blackline master).

Organizing Conferences

Even though you will conference with numerous children every day, you will not be able to conference with all of your students every day. Make sure you do not focus only on the prolific writers who constantly seek you out or the sleeve-tugging students who are constantly in need of assistance. Instead, try to focus on one small group of students, or a table group each day, ensuring that within a week or so, you will have visited with each student.

You may want to create a small chart to indicate which group or table you will be conferencing with on that day. On the top of the chart, tape paper clips that can hold a handful of student names, colored cards representing the table groups in your classroom, or some other organizational mechanism indicating which group you will be spending time with on that day. Introduce the poster to students, showing them how it will work with one table/group meeting with you every day for conferences. (Note: You will not be conferencing with the students as a group; those are simply the students that you will be working with that day.)

This system clearly lets students know when their turn for conferencing is, both so that they can be properly prepared, and also so that they know when they are not to approach you. Teach students how to support one another and to look to their peers for assistance when you are unavailable. Students who are scheduled for conferences on that day will also begin to take on responsibility for redirecting their peers: "Sorry. It's our turn to conference today. You'll get your turn tomorrow." Every day, flip over the card (or have the Student Classroom Assistant flip it over) and identify which group you will work with. Try not to assign each group to a day of the week as there are uneven numbers of Mondays and Fridays, and some days, assemblies or specials take away time normally dedicated to writing. This structure will ensure that all students receive their fair share of writing instruction. You will also find that as students look to their peers for assistance, you have more focused time in the conferences.

Formal Assessment

To be effective in making instructional decisions on a regular basis, teachers have to know exactly what students already know and what they need to learn. Formal assessments not only inform instruction; they are also tools to report students' learning to parents, administrators, and policy makers. Formal assessments are more than just report cards and standardized tests; they also include assessment tools such as running records and checklists.

Report Cards

The teaching staff at the Manhattan New School in New York City struggles with the same concerns many teachers hold about report cards: How can teachers record the complicated process of learning, recognizing student growth at so many different points on the learning continuum, when they are limited by a document that uses a single letter to represent the volumes of learning children have done? The answer may be just as Joan Servis

(1999) suggested when she shared that she attempts "to give them [report cards] some validity through rubrics and other self-assessment tools" (113). It must be recognized that a report card is but one element in a complex web of assessment tools that provides a profile of a student. The use of rubrics to support the grades presented through a report card is a helpful supplement. See the section in this chapter on the construction and use of rubrics for more information.

> The Board of Education report card wouldn't work for us. It did not reflect what we believed to be important about students' academic and social growth. We know that learning is fascinating, complicated stuff. But the report card set out vague categories and, by limiting the number of assessment areas, gave the impression that learning is easy. (Hindley 1996, 136–137)

In order to increase your observational efficiency, you might consider organizing your ongoing assessment practices around the elements addressed on the report card. As you engage in your regular observations and anecdotal note taking, you may choose to include a "focus for observation" each week, in addition to the informal observations you are making as you notice things and record anecdotal information. For example, if the report card states, "Uses quotation marks correctly in dialogue," instead of trying to assess all of your students at report card time, indicate that as a "focus for observation" for yourself for one week, and record student progress on that skill as you conference with each child that week. If you notice that certain children consistently demonstrate proficiency, you do not need to take the time to reassess this later. On the other hand, if you note that some children are struggling, you have time to provide instruction and then reassess those children on that skill later.

When sending out report cards, consider including copies of the rubrics you use in assigning grades, as well as any literacy checklists and narrative statements you have completed in order to best represent each child's progress as a learner.

Rubrics

A rubric is a device that teachers can use to clearly identify specific criteria for learning. For example, an item on a report card stating "Uses punctuation correctly" becomes more useful to teachers, students, and parents when it is more clearly defined. Using this example, teachers might establish a rubric stating the specific punctuation that has been introduced and identifying performance ranges correlated with grades. For example "consistent use" receives an A; "somewhat consistent use" receives a B; "inconsistent use" receives a C; "infrequent use" receives a D; and so on. Although this rubric may still be considered somewhat vague, it is more clearly defined than the original statement found on the report card, "Uses punctuation correctly." The more specific a rubric is, the more helpful, but only to the point that it is still manageable and useful.

Establishing rubrics such as this one not only enables teachers to assign grades more easily, but it also provides students and parents with clear explanations of grades. It would be wise for teachers to consider working with students for classroom specific rubrics, or together with grade level, school, or district teams to come up with rubrics for the different elements that appear on a report card.

> My colleagues and I compiled a reading rubric, but we found it difficult to use because some of the indicators, such as "makes relevant contributions," were ambiguous. I wanted a rubric the students and I could use, one that incorporated child-friendly language and listed reasonable criteria for evaluation. Because I put such emphasis on student self-assessment, it was especially important that students could use it easily to evaluate their own progress, so I asked them to help me design a rubric for our November parent conferences. In our discussions, we referred to the district report card to make sure we included all important areas. Then we selected the indicators by vote, and now we use this rubric each trimester. Students also refer to it when filling out self-evaluation forms for the November and March parent conferences. (Servis 1999, 78)

Checklists

Checklists are valuable records of student progress over time. The most useful checklists are those that are recycled and reused throughout the school year. A checklist provides students, teachers, and parents with a clear overview of what is expected of that child as a learner. They provide a continuum of teaching and learning that can be used to evaluate both teaching and learning and to direct future instruction. Depending on your needs, it may be appropriate to use checklists with only some of your students, rather than the entire class. Sample checklists can be found in the appendix.

Rather than using a brand-new checklist for each assessment period, reuse the same form, using a different colored pen for each term. If the checklist is a good one, it will provide a complete continuum, representing the span of literacy skills and strategies that your students will be expected to demonstrate proficiency in by the end of the year. Learning should be viewed as an ongoing process and assessment should reflect that.

A system like this one allows teachers to better monitor the progress students are making over time. It also provides a direction for future instruction, whether it is in the form of introducing new content and strategies or in revisiting them. Similar to report card assessments, the use of checklists is much more manageable if they are filled out on an ongoing basis. Choose a couple of elements each week and pull students regularly for "mini-assessment" opportunities, focusing solely on those elements.

Modified Oral Reading Records

Even at the intermediate level, there is nothing better than an actual running record taken as a child reads aloud to assess your students' behaviors and progress as readers. Effective assessment is that which most closely parallels the task being assessed, and nothing is more valuable in determining a child's reading progress than sitting down and listening to him or her read. True running records may not be appropriate or feasible at the intermediate level due to the complexity of texts and rate of reading, but recording a sampling of behaviors and miscues provides a profile of sorts, allowing the teacher to better understand each child as a reader and to provide productive follow-up instruction.

It must also be recognized that intermediate students have often reached a point of fluency in their development wherein their oral reading may be weaker than their silent reading. Think of yourself as a reader: Do you do a better job reading orally or silently? When we become proficient, fluent readers, our minds and eyes can work more quickly than our mouths, resulting in less accurate reading of text. This ability to sub-vocalize must be taken into account when assessing and evaluating students' oral reading behaviors, but there is still no replacement for the benefits derived from actually hearing a student read aloud. It is through doing so that teachers learn which students are word callers, word skippers, mumblers, or those who over-rely on phonics when reading. In listening to what children do as they read, and how they do it,

> *In an effort to efficiently and effectively record the behaviors of more fluent readers in an unobtrusive fashion, I sit to the right of a child (I am right-handed, so sitting on a student's left side and taking notes would result in slightly turning my back to him or her) and jot my notes on a small index card. On this card, I record the student's name, the date, the title and genre of the text, and then, after a brief conversation, a few notes about the child's comprehension of the text thus far. I then invite the child to read a bit of the text and I simply listen in, working to identify strengths and areas of need the child demonstrates. After listening to a couple of paragraphs and jotting down any observations of strategy use, miscues, and other behaviors worth recording, I choose one or two that will be worth discussing, and we engage in a brief conversation about that child as a reader. As in writing conferences, I try to very clearly identify both strengths of the reader as well as specific strategies or areas in need of attention. These conferences are powerful tools for learning about individual students which then allow me to provide appropriate and timely whole group, small group, and individual instruction, based on students' needs. —Lisa*

we are able to step inside their minds temporarily, getting a glimpse into that child's world as a reader, working either effectively or ineffectively to navigate through text, working towards comprehension.

A running record is a shorthand method of recording a student's reading of a text. The system was invented by Marie Clay (1993) as a standardized method of accurately recording reading behavior by noting all the behaviors that students engage in as they make their way through a sample of about 100 words of text. It will take a few hours of practice—about the total time it would take for you to take one or two running records on each child in your classroom—for a teacher to become comfortable and automatic with taking a running record. Once you establish this comfort level, you are in control of an invaluable assessment tool.

Take running records regularly on both familiar and unfamiliar texts. A running record on a familiar text allows you to reflect on your instruction as well as a student's reading behavior. A running record on an unfamiliar text provides a pure picture of the strategies that child has ownership of independent of any instruction related to that text.

Running records are most effective when you take them regularly, rather than only at the beginning and end of the year. An easy way to ensure that this happens is to take one formal running record on one child every day. If you have identified a Student Classroom Assistant, it would be logical to find a few minutes at some point in the day to take a record on that child. Finding a time in your day to establish this ongoing assessment routine allows you to take one record on every child every four to six weeks.

Running records can also be used in your reading groups on a daily basis. As mentioned previously in this chapter, you can take a simple running record on the previous day's text at the beginning of a small group reading lesson as a quick way to determine whether the text level they are working on is appropriate and to do a strategy use check.

Either way, running records provide teachers with very specific information about a student's current strengths and needs as a developing reader. You can use this information to your advantage when creating future instruction.

Other Published Assessment Tools and Devices

Many schools and districts require certain assessments across the grade levels, and many teachers select their own outside assessment tools. Evaluate these assessments carefully, analyzing their purpose and value. It is important as we look at assessment tools that we reflect on the two questions: Why am I doing this? How is it good for children? Assessments used in the classroom should be utilized in order to support the teaching that goes on within those walls. We need to ask ourselves, "How will this information help me to be a better teacher?" If we are unable to answer that question with a logical response, we need to re-evaluate the use of that assessment tool.

Standardized Tests

Many teachers feel standardized tests rarely give them any information they are not already aware of. Teachers know which students will succeed and which will fail because they have engaged in purposeful assessment all along and are well aware of the strengths

Section 1

and weaknesses of their learners (Servis 1999). Standardized tests can often be a significant source of stress for teachers and students. Even though many educators feel they are not accurate reflections of student learning, standardized tests are here to stay. Knowing this, it is in teachers' best interest to attend to standardized tests in as positive fashion as possible. *A Teacher's Guide to Standardized Reading Tests* is an invaluable text that helps teachers to "live thoughtfully in the presence of tests and to do so without selling their souls" (Calkins, Montgomery, and Santman 1998, 8).

Following the district or state's curriculum should ensure teachers that their students will experience a reasonable degree of success on standardized tests as the two should parallel one another to some degree. Looking beyond the mere content of the test, teachers must take time to consider the actual reading and writing skills that are unique to the test-taking genre and required for a student's success. Knowing that the multiple choice and written response formats are often quite dissimilar from the more authentic literacy experiences a child will have in an effective literacy classroom, it is important to consider how teachers can support students to be successful in this somewhat artificial situation.

> Take a practice test yourself. What strategies are most useful for responding to the test questions? Teach those to your students. (Routman 2003, 111)

Using the gradual release of responsibility theory of teaching and learning, a teacher who wants students to perform well will take the time to engage in modeled, shared, and guided instruction on how to navigate this new genre and its unique vocabulary set successfully. Preparing for standardized tests in this manner would be far more productive than the traditional test preparation model, as "asking children to take one practice test after another might reinforce ineffective test-taking strategies" (Calkins, Montgomery, and Santman 1998, 70). Teachers may find that conferencing with students after they take practice tests is beneficial. In a conference, students will reveal the strategies they used to arrive at an answer. You may discover that those strategies may not be very appropriate. A child who consistently chooses the first answer that looks good to him or her will certainly not fare well. It is the teacher's responsibility to model the inner thought processes that accompany test taking, to maneuver through test questions with students, and to support them as they develop appropriate test-taking strategies of their own.

Another consideration is the actual test-taking situation. Instead of having students show up on test day to a completely foreign environment characterized by isolated desks set up in rows that present a stark contrast to their usually comforting classroom, follow Kathy Doyle's (in Calkins 1999) example. After explaining the parameters of the test-taking situation, invite students to determine the best test-taking setting for themselves. Allow them to try out the different locations within the classroom to determine which area will be most conducive to successful performance.

Teacher responsibilities related to standardized testing are not over once the tests are boxed up and shipped off to be scored. It is important for teachers to consider seriously the outcome and results of the assessments. Where are the areas of relative strength and weakness across the student population? After identifying these, the teaching staff of the school (not just of the teachers at the grade level being tested) should take on the responsibility to work more aggressively in those areas. This is not a suggestion to teach to the test—it is a suggestion for teachers to be more aware of where instructional time needs to

In one district in New Jersey, teachers and administrators decided to put all their energy into a test preparation curriculum for their students. They followed a program designed specifically for the test their students would take. Within two years, their students had the highest scores in the area on that reading test. The sad ending to the story is that when these same kids went to high school, one third of them had to be placed in remedial reading classes. It was as if the children had been given steroids to artificially boost their short-term performance. (Calkins, Montgomery, and Santman 1998, 47)

Finding the Time

The most effective teachers constantly evaluate students' learning and needs as they are teaching. When I work in classrooms, I integrate teaching and evaluating all day long. (Routman 2003, 305)

be spent for students to be successful.

It is important to make sure that every minute of the school day counts toward assessment, instruction, or learning of some sort. The tiny windows of time that once added up to hours of misused opportunities could easily be dedicated to assessment. The following are some strategies for integrating assessment into the school day.

One simple way I found to keep up with assessment was to have the Student Classroom Assistant carry out my assessment basket during recess, during which I was required to monitor my students. In this basket, I would keep the current checklist or the pieces I would need to do a simple assessment such as a sight word identification task. As the other children were running around, I could work for a few minutes with one student without being interrupted by other children. Naturally, I could not use this time for very intense assessments that would require my full attention, disallowing me to monitor my students, nor could I successfully pull every child at this point. However, there were always some students who had no problem taking a few minutes of their recess time to work with me. Others would not take very kindly to this, so their assessment time always fell within the normal school activities inside our classroom. —Lisa

Section 1

When children are working independently, the teacher has the perfect opportunity to work with students for assessment purposes. Whether it is through observation of work behaviors, a reading or writing conference, or a more formal assessment tool, be sure to take advantage of these windows of opportunity for assessment. If you wait until report card time, you will be overwhelmed and find that you may have lost instructional time in teaching information that your students already knew or were not quite ready to learn.

Keeping Track of It All

It is clear that both formal and informal assessments are of great value to teachers in monitoring student progress and in informing instruction, but assessment may well be worthless if it is not organized and maintained in a manner in which the teacher can readily access and use the information. There are a number of time- and space-saving tips that will allow you to physically organize your records for prompt retrieval and use of formal and informal assessment data.

Consider setting up assessment folders in a hanging file crate—a small one on wheels will prove to be especially handy. Designate a hanging file folder for each child, and within each, place two regular pocket folders. Dedicate one of these folders for you and one for the child. In your folder keep the assessment documents you want to maintain on each child (such as running records, pages holding anecdotal notes specific to that child, checklists, selected writing samples) and place all other documents (such as other writing samples, projects, or other items that are completed throughout a given week) into the child's folder.

At the end of every week or two, take a few minutes to look through each assessment folder with each student. Encourage each child to choose one piece (possibly with some influence from you) that he or she feels best represents his or her learning for the week. Staple the piece of writing to the inside cover of the folder along with a note identifying your reflections on that student as a learner in general or in reference to that particular document. For example, you may note: "Julie has made great progress in punctuating her stories. Not only is there evidence of dialogue in her narratives, she is also incorporating quotation marks and appropriate punctuation inside the quotes, including commas." With the exception of writing samples and other documents you select for your assessment folder, send the rest of the papers home with students.

Using an organizational system such as this is going to support both teachers and students in several ways. First, teachers will have an opportunity to look at each child through a more holistic lens as they review with children the work they have done over the past week or so. Reviewing information on an ongoing basis will also immediately fuel teachers' instruction of their students and make conferences and cumulative assessments on report cards much more manageable. This system will help students as they sit side by side with the teacher considering themselves as learners reflecting on the assessment tools and artifacts within the folder.

Assessment is imperative if instruction is to be optimally effective and efficient. Remember, the most effective mode of assessment is the one that works best for you.

Sharing It All with Others

The primary purpose of assessment is generally to inform the teacher, but it is also helpful and necessary to share that information with others at times. Suggestions have been made throughout the chapter for how to share with students through reading, writing, and progress conferences, but it is also important to consider how to most effectively share with parents and fellow staff members.

Sharing with fellow staff members requires that you are fully knowledgeable of the student's academic and behavioral development in very clear terms. Documentation is essential, especially when communicating with specialists and special services teams. Following the suggestions in this chapter will be beneficial in ensuring that the communication is productive, precise, and clear.

Parent conferences are an important undertaking and should not be hastily or poorly planned. Teachers who have worked to assess on a regular and ongoing basis, as has been suggested in this chapter, will find that conferences are comfortable and natural opportunities to celebrate student progress and to share concerns and goals.

Some suggestions for parent or caregiver conferences include:

1. **Have a schedule clearly posted outside of your classroom so that parents are informed.** Be sure to do your best to schedule conferences that may run longer than the allotted period at the end of the conference session or at a different time.

2. **As parents wait, consider having pen and paper handy for them to jot down notes or questions.** Sarah has found success in sending home a survey before conferences, asking parents to think about their goals, hopes, and questions related to their child's progress.

3. **Have additional paper and pens available where the conference will be held** so that parents can write down notes during the conference.

4. **Consider keeping a small timer with you so that conferences are timely and do not run over.** If you choose to use the classroom clock to keep track of time, organize the conference so that you are seated with the clock in clear view behind the caregiver as you are looking at him or her so that you do not have to turn around in order to view it.

5. **Hold conferences at a table or in a comfortable setting** where you and the parent are seated as equals, collaborating on the student's progress in learning.

6. **If it is possible, have students involved in conferences**, sharing what they have learned and where they see themselves going next.

7. **Enter the conference fully prepared yourself.** This means that you need to have documentation of your assertions in the form of the formal and informal assessments and record-keeping outlined in this chapter.

8. **Enjoy these opportunities to work closely with parents.** Take time to recognize and celebrate the strengths of each child as you speak with parents, as well as note specific areas of need or growth. In difficult conferences, work diligently to maintain the parent as an ally as you work together to support the student.

> ### Efficiency and Effectiveness Task
>
> #### Assessing Your Assesments
> Reflect on your current assessment routines. What are you doing and what are you using? Is your routine working? Are the tools you are using helpful? Identify three things that you will work to continue doing or change in your assessment practice in order to make it a more efficient and effective one.

Section 2: Setting the Tone for the Rest of the Year

The ultimate degree of success a teacher and his or her students will experience in any given year can be measured in part through what happens during the first few weeks of the school year. Fountas and Pinnell (1996) borrowed the words of the New Zealand Board of Education, reminding teachers that "even the most lavishly appointed classroom may turn to shambles" if routines for using it have not been established. It is important for teachers to take time at the beginning of the year to establish the routines of peaceful and productive co-existence within the walls of their classrooms.

The time that teachers invest in their efforts to establish an efficiently run classroom is well worth it. Dedicating a significant amount of time to the teaching of routines before children are expected to work independently will yield greater and more productive instructional time later (Fountas and Pinnell 1996).

Of course the timelines for establishing a classroom environment that runs smoothly will differ. It is important to base timelines on a group's previous experience with a more independent work-oriented structure, overall class maturity and chemistry, the grade level, and the teacher's current level of comfort as he or she works to release greater responsibility to students. Even the same teacher should expect variance from year to year as he or she works to establish a structure that will allow for successful independent work opportunities. Every year he or she will be a slightly different teacher due to another year's worth of experiences and will also have an entirely different group of children representing a unique set of strengths and needs.

Chapter 4

Establishing Ongoing Routines

> Teachers who initially take sufficient time to establish a classroom community with predictable routines, clear expectations, warm personal relationships, and a climate of respect reap the benefits all year long and, ultimately, wind up with more time for teaching. While it sounds easy to set up a classroom for success, it requires skill and experience–and firmness and patience. (Routman 2000, 541)

The first days of school can make or break you. Based on what a teacher does or does not do, a teacher will either have or not have an effective classroom for the rest of the year. What happens on the first days of school will be an accurate indicator of your success for the rest of the school year" (Wong 1998, 3). It is within this window of time that you can take the opportunity to introduce students to the expectations that you have for them. Rather than establish a long list of rules that you dictate and students follow without question, you and your students can work as a group over a period of several weeks to organize the system that will carry you through the year, making slight modifications as the need arises. This fosters an environment where all may learn successfully and peacefully together.

Rules vs. Expectations

There is a clear difference between a *rule* and an *expectation*. A rule is something that one can break and violate; an expectation is something that one can work to live up to in a supported environment. "Think of rules as 'standard operating procedures' or 'agreements.' They are descriptions of the way people agree to work together in a classroom. They are based not on your 'authority' as the teacher but on the social conventions essential for a productive, harmonious classroom that enable students to do their best work and allow others to do their best" (Fountas and Pinnell 2001, 103).

There is a considerable difference between a classroom governed by rules and one that functions smoothly as students and teachers live up to joint expectations as they follow procedures that have been established as routines. As you reflect on the structures you are coordinating in an effort to support the smooth operation of your classroom, consider whether you will choose to dictate a set of rules to be followed, or whether you will work with your students to establish the manner in which you co-exist in the classroom. It is interesting to note that as responsibility is released to students as they work to establish their classroom guidelines, they often come up with the same or even more structured expectations for behavior than you would have as their teacher. The more students are involved in the establishment of the manners of existence within their classroom, the more accountable you can expect them to be for living up to those standards.

If you choose to have rules in your classroom, they should be reserved for the absolutes,

Chapter 4: Establishing Ongoing Routines

and there should be no more than three to five total. Those rules should be your rules or those devised by your students—not a prefabricated list of rules for behavior. It is also important to reserve rules for behavioral guidelines and not academic ones. For example, "Do your homework every day" should not be a rule (Wong 1998).

You may find that a finite number of rules are necessary in your classroom—both for your students as well as for your own comfort. It is important to remember to keep these rules brief and absolute. "No talking without raising your hand!" is not a good rule as it is not true all the time. Also take care to phrase your rules in as positive a voice as possible. Most of the time, the "Don't do..." version of a rule is not as effective as its positive counterpart. Instead, try to focus your energies and instruction on "Do...." For example, "Don't talk without raising your hand" could be restated to a more positive and true statement "Do wait your turn before speaking." Restating this rule in a more general way also lends itself to a more appropriate application. Students need to wait for their turn in a whole group or small group lesson, in a partner conversation,

> *As I think about my past experiences as a teacher when I have posted a list of rules in my classroom, I realize that I cannot think of a single instance wherein a child did or did not do something as a result of that list. I have never seen a child go up to a list of posted rules and check it to make sure that he or she was not breaking any of them before he or she acted. I would often direct students to the chart, "Go read number three!" I would rattle off as an infraction was made. The child would dutifully march off, read the rule, and then go right back to work not having learned much and probably destined to break the same rule again.*
>
> *I would say the most successful year I had in terms of behavior within my classroom was the year I did not establish a single rule. I bought a poster labeled "Classroom Rules," and after putting it up on the wall, intending to create the class rules together, I literally forgot about it altogether until the last day of school when we were taking everything down. One of my students grabbed it and said, "Hey Ms. D, what's this thing for?" That was the year I had very high and very clear expectations for everything that went on in my classroom. We had routines and procedures for everything—but no "rules." —Lisa*

and in conferences with their teacher—raising their hands before speaking in any of these situations would be unnecessary. Consider how you help your students develop responsibility for their behavior. A dictatorship is not the most successful model for running a group of children. If you want children to be responsible for their behavior, you must help them to do so. Children will quite regularly respond to the unfailing expectations you establish if they are clearly communicated, along with the appropriate coinciding procedures, routines, and patterns of behavior.

Teachers should begin every year with a list of expectations that they will hold for their students. Again, a handful of rules may be appropriate, but if this turns into an unmanageable list, it will not benefit you or your students. What is it that children need to learn about functioning as part of a group and, in particular, within the classroom? It is logical to spend a considerable amount of time and energy helping students function within a potentially overwhelming situation. The routines you establish will be a phenomenal help in assisting students as they work to make good choices. Children must learn how to work on their own and with others and how to care for, respect, and share the materials available to them. It is also important that they have an understanding of some of the logistical components inherent to functioning successfully within a larger community—this includes the individual classroom as well as the entire school as a unit.

In working to establish a productive classroom environment, the first four weeks are of critical importance. During that time frame, there are specific windows of time during which a classroom teacher needs to focus on slightly different elements as he or she works to establish the climate and routines that will support both the teacher and students for the duration of the year: before school, the first day, the first, second, third, and fourth weeks of school and beyond. This chapter outlines a portion of the routines, expectations, guidelines for using materials, and relationship-building activities that teachers may want to address during the first critical weeks of school. The next chapter provides a more in-depth view of how to integrate these suggestions into the first four weeks of school, including the time just before the year begins to establish a solid foundation in your classroom.

Do not use these suggestions as a rigid sequence of events; the order will always be slightly different as the vast majority of instruction comes about in direct response to children's needs. The items in this section are not an exhaustive list, but each is essential. They (and any other items you find a need for) should appear in your lesson plans consistently in the beginning of the year and as needed throughout the year. Make sure to take advantage of teachable moments when they present themselves, knowing that "Student achievement at the end of the year is directly related to the degree to which the teacher establishes good control of the classroom procedures in the very first week of the school year" (Wong 1998, 4). Whatever time you invest up front will support all of your efforts for the remainder of the year.

Organizing and Managing Your Classroom for Optimal Effectiveness: Ongoing Routines

The following are some general categories to consider when working toward organizing and managing your classroom for optimal effectiveness. These should be introduced gradually within the first weeks of school with the greatest emphasis placed on teaching routines. From that point on, you can expend more time and energy on assessment and instruction, but plan to revisit each of these as the need arises. You may want to use a chart similar to the Teaching Routines Checklist (see appendix for full blackline master), to keep track of which routines you introduced and revisited.

It is important to begin with the end in mind (Covey 1989), so determine for yourself how and to what degree you want your students to function independently. The exact time to introduce each routine will depend on your unique situation each year.

Teaching Routines

It is important to spend a considerable amount of time up front to establish the routines in your classroom that will result in a smoothly-run operation. The more time you spend working to manage your environment effectively, the more time you will have available to yourself and your students for instruction as the year progresses.

> **Efficiency and Effectiveness Task**
>
> ### Anticipating Trouble Spots
> Reflect for a moment on "trouble spots" you anticipate within your classroom. Consider potential or past areas of trouble throughout the school day and create a list of the things you are worried about or that take away from the efficiency and effectiveness of your classroom. We will refer to this list again at the end of the chapter.

Using Materials

The following are some suggestions for teaching your students to find, use, and put away materials throughout the day.

- **Where to get paper.** Passing out paper for writing tasks on a daily basis can cut into precious instructional time. Make sure that every student in your classroom has a writing notebook to use for a variety of purposes. Be sure to make additional notebooks and other writing paper (lined, unlined, partially lined, yellow, white, newsprint) available to students as they need it. Store the paper in a location where students can easily get whatever they need. It may take some effort to teach students how to pull paper from the top of the stack as well as how to reorganize the stack if it needs to be.

- **Where to get pens/pencils.** Each student should have two pens and/or pencils in his or her desk at all times. There is no need for more or fewer if these resources are available elsewhere in the classroom for replacement purposes. At the beginning of the year, establish this as a standard by stopping frequently for a pen or pencil check: "Everyone stop! Take out your pens and pencils. You need two of each. Anything extra needs to go back to our extra supplies section." If you do this frequently enough, it will soon become a habit for students to return extra writing utensils immediately as they find them, rather than building a growing collection in their desk.

To organize the "extra materials" and to avoid the hoarding of pens or the constant breakage of pencil tips that goes on in many classrooms, start out with three cups, each a different color. Use one colored cup for pens, another cup (red for "Stop! Don't use these!") as a depository for broken or need-to-be-sharpened pencils, and the third colored cup (green for "Go! These are ready to use!") for ready-to-go pencils. Avoid sharpening pencils during the school day as that would not be a good use of instructional time. Instead, ask a child in your class to sharpen them all before school starts. Broken or missing pencils provide students with an excuse for not writing. A small amount of time dedicated to establishing good habits saves far greater time as the year progresses.

On the first day of school, make sure each student has two pencils, and place the remaining pencils in the ready-to-go pencil cup. If a child brings a fancy pen or pencil that might cause a problem, suggest keeping it at home or permitting it to be added to the shared stock as the intent here is to maintain joint custody of all the materials. As mentioned above, several times daily for the first several weeks, and every few days thereafter, have everyone do a pen/pencil search for about fifteen seconds—anyone who finds extra pencils can simply deposit them in the appropriate cup. This establishes having only two pens and pencils at a time as a habit, guaranteeing plenty to go around.

- **Where to get a book.** Begin teaching students about the classroom library on the first day of school. Organize your books into baskets according to themes, topics, or authors in order to make them more accessible. Having hundreds of books on shelves makes it hard to find the one you want and even harder to return it to its proper location.

It would be wise not to introduce all of your books at once, as this might be quite overwhelming. Instead, introduce one basket of twenty or so books on a single topic, all with an identical sticker on the front cover or other identifying mark you have added that will help children return books to the proper location. In a few days, introduce another basket of books with a new common focus and matching sticker. It is easy for children to match the books up with only two options. Gradually increase the number of books and baskets, and add to the baskets as the year goes on. By the end of the year, the shelves will be full, and students will have opportunities to visit with new texts throughout the year. Once students have been introduced to the system, it should be easy for them to borrow and return books without any assistance or direction.

A good rule is to allow students to always have one book in their desk for immediate access. You also may want to allow children to have access to the books that are in the box designated for their reading group. Within the first three days of school, teach students that they should always have at least one book on hand at any given time. As long as the class is not engaged in a directed activity, it is acceptable for students to switch one book for another one whenever they like. With proper introduction, support, and frequent checks (multiple times per day, initially) to make sure that every child has the appropriate number of texts readily available, no child will ever have to ask "Where do I get a book?"

- **How to find a just-right book.** Make sure to have frequent conferences with children, ensuring that they are able to identify too hard, too easy, and just-right books for themselves—for some this is easier than for others. A good approach is the popular Goldilocks strategy (Ohlihausen and Jepsin 1992). In making a link to the popular fairy tale in which Goldilocks is repeatedly finding things that are too hot, too small, or too soft, you can help children realize that every book is not a just-right read for every reader. Through individual conferences, you can help children develop an awareness of books that are just right. Another method that works with some more fluent readers is the five-finger method (Veatch 1959). As students read a selection with about 100 words, they pop up a finger each time they encounter a word they do not know. If they reach five, that book may be too hard for them to read independently. So that children can always find a book on their independent level, you may want to create book boxes for individuals or for each reading group, containing a collection of just-right books.

- **How to teach respect for books.** You may want to spend a considerable amount of time on proper book handling skills. Use dramatizations, by yourself or with students, to show them how to hold a book, turn the pages, and share it with a friend. Also, every time a new book or basket arrives, look at every one of them with students. "Oh, wow! This one's about...Alex, you will really like this one because..." This advertises each title, getting children excited about them.

Managing Noise Levels

Many teachers have tried to manage the noise level in their classrooms by requesting children to use six-inch or twelve-inch voices or by teaching them to monitor volume and adjusting it according to each situation. Directing students to use whisper voices may not be as effective as it is not always possible or appropriate to whisper (Everston, Emmer, and Worsham 2003).

Even if you provide guidelines, sometimes noise becomes bothersome when students are working independently—they are unable to concentrate due to the volume of their peers' voices. It is in your best interest to teach students how to handle this situation by role-playing how to approach another student and saying, "I am trying to... and I can't because you are a little too noisy. Can you please work a little more quietly so that I can get my work done?" This is exactly how adults are expected to handle the same situation, so why not teach children how to do it as well?

You can also teach a sophisticated group of students to think about their volume from other students' perspective. For example, you could teach children at the Listening Station to check with the students around them as they turn the machine on: "Is this too loud? Can you still get your work done?"

Getting Help

It is in teachers' best interest to provide complete directions and instructions and to expect that students can successfully work on their own. However, this is not always the case, and an effective and proactive teacher will anticipate this and organize routines to support students who are seeking help or attention.

- **How to handle mistakes.** Effective teachers spend a great deal of time teaching children that mistakes are acceptable. It is through making mistakes and then learning from them that we grow as learners. When modeling reading, writing, or other behaviors, a teacher should never *intentionally* make a mistake. Providing a model of something requires, inherently, that it be done correctly; otherwise, it is not a demonstration of that skill or strategy. Mistakes happen, though, and when they do as we model, we need to recognize that a mistake has been made and point out the nature of it to students. The behavior we are modeling is that "Mistakes are accepted here! They are a natural part of learning!" In fact, teachers should be more concerned if they are *not* seeing mistakes. Making no errors indicates that students are not taking risks that are essential to learning and growth.

    In teaching children to handle mistakes, it is important, especially at the beginning of the year, to minimize corrective actions or aggressive instruction when students make errors so that students do not feel uncomfortable making mistakes. Once students realize that the classroom is a place where errors and mistakes are not a cause for punishment or embarrassment, you can begin to work to use their mistakes to inform future learning. Initially, however, your goal needs to be geared towards helping children move to develop tolerance of their mistakes.

- **How to manage too many questions.** Teach children to ask the Student Classroom Assistant for help or to "Ask three before you ask me." (Before asking the teacher a question, the students should go to three of their peers for assistance. Use role-play to teach students to ask three of their peers for help before approaching you.) You will find that you are disrupted far less frequently and that students become more independent. Spencer Kagan (1992) suggests a similar strategy. When students work in cooperative groups, they can collaborate, working together to answer questions and solve problems. If they are unable to find the solution by working together, they may ask for help but only by collectively raising their hands—every member must hold up his or her hand, indicating that they have tried but exhausted their resources and truly need help. Using any of these strategies, you will greatly reduce interruptions to your day at the same time your students will develop appropriate independent work behaviors.

- **How to address students copying others' work.** Copying someone else's work is a very effective coping strategy when assigned work is too challenging or perceived to be too difficult. Unfortunately, it is also illegal. Instead of focusing on the "copy-er," direct your attention to the "copy-ee." Teach the second child to turn his or her paper over and ask the offender if he or she needs help. The child can then help his or her peer just the way a teacher would—never tell the answer; just help the student find it on his or her own.

Getting Students' Attention

Every teacher needs to implement an emergency response signal that will result in complete and automatic attention. The best signals to get attention are those that are of the call and response nature. The teacher engages in behavior signaling a need for students' immediate attention, and the students respond in a way that requires them to stop whatever they are doing. For example, the teacher may say "1, 2, 3" and the students join in on the next line, "Look at me!" while looking up at the teacher (Everston, Emmer, and Worsham 2003). Many teachers use the one finger-on-the-lips-one finger-in-the-air maneuver that is supposed to work somewhat like the wave at a sporting event. This method may take too long and you may end up begging for the attention of the children who are unaware. Other teachers have used the lights-off system, but some children often continue working or talking. A variation of this might be to flash the lights once or twice and then start a countdown from five or ten, ending with "3, 2, 1, zip!" While saying "zip," have children pretend to zip up their lips (like a zipper) and direct their attention to the teacher (Everston, Emmer, and Worsham 2003). Another method that works quite well is the clap-clap, clap-clap-clap (two slow claps, three fast claps) for attention. This method simultaneously taps into the auditory, visual, and kinesthetic systems. It is important to practice whatever system you decide on again and again throughout the first days of school; however, there are a few guidelines to adhere to:

- **Always use the same system.** Changing methods or clapping patterns to make it double as a mathematics activity will only cause confusion.

- **Demand immediate and complete attention and then follow up with immediate, succinct, and precise information.** If you don't provide your message immediately, or if you go on for too long, students will make the choice not to listen.

Working Inside the Classroom (Alone and with Others)

In an effective literacy classroom, students have a great deal of responsibility for their own behavior and learning. In releasing this responsibility to students, teachers must anticipate potential problems and spend time teaching specific behaviors and responses to avoid such situations.

- **What to do if you are finished.** If you spend time during the first few weeks of school supporting students on how to work independently, "I'm done! What do I do now?" is a statement you will never hear again. Teach children that once they finish a task, they can move onto an approved independent activity. At the beginning of the year, this may include "Finish your work, then read from your book at your table." As the year goes on and children demonstrate the ability to work independently in such a fashion, you might allow them to read elsewhere in the classroom, or engage in another independent task. Gradually expand their range of choices as they display their ability to handle it. This model follows and supports the gradual release of responsibility that will support your students as they gradually take on the role of a responsible learner.

- **How to sit in the group area.** This goes far beyond the "Cross your legs like a pretzel" mantra often heard in classrooms. The group area in an intermediate classroom may include students sitting on the floor, on chairs, on couches, or other surfaces, and how to go about doing so requires the establishment of relevant routines. With students on the floor, work to help them understand why it is important to sit all the way down, unless they are all the way in the back of the group. Teach children to look over their shoulder to see if they are in the back or if someone is sitting behind them to ensure that that person can see clearly, just as we would as adults.

    Also talk about the importance of keeping their hands off the floor and turning their body so that they are facing the speaker head on, instead of sitting cock-eyed and craning their necks around to see. If the speaker moves, the listener has to shift too. A final expectation is to teach children to come to the floor in a calm fashion and "shuffle up" on the mat, filling in any space between themselves and the person in front of them so that everyone is close together but not so close that children have knees in their backs. Avoid putting marks or boxes on the floor to direct children where to sit. When you get on a crowded bus, you do not look for a square with your name on it; you look around for a place to sit where you can fit comfortably and will not be next to a potentially troublesome person. It is important to teach students these real-life skills that they can carry with them beyond school. Also avoid embarrassing students who run to the floor by sending them back to their seats to do it again. Instead, remind them of the dangers of rushing. Pretty soon, other children will repeat your words instead of tattling. With a gentle reminder of "Don't forget to think about how you're going to come to the floor" before inviting them to the floor, students will have no trouble responding appropriately.

- **How to sit in your chair.** It is important to teach students how to sit properly in their chairs. They need to know that "four on the floor" is the way to go.

- **How to ask someone to move out of your way.** It is much more beneficial to be proactive about this and teach it in isolation, rather than to wait for a squabble to break out and then demand apologies. Role-play is extremely

> *It has been my experience that students who tip their chairs are usually not being defiant. More than likely, they are bored and are looking for a way to entertain themselves. In this case, I take a closer look at what I am doing than at what the child is doing. A child seriously engaged in the task of learning will be quite unable to divert his or her mental energies to balancing his or her chair on two legs.* —Lisa

beneficial in teaching children how to handle such situations. Children quickly learn to tap the child gently and say, "Excuse me, please. Did you know that you just stepped on my coat/ran into me/are blocking my view? Could you move over, please?" The other child is taught to say, "Oh my! Here, is that better?" or "Oh my! Are you OK? I didn't mean to…" Try not to focus all of your attention on the instigator, as the other child also has much to learn about how to handle such situations properly.

> *Other than initially, I very, very rarely direct my children. Instead I teach them to be responsible for asking one other to move. That way, they learn that it is their responsibility. —Lisa*

- **How to form a line.** Standing in front of a group of children, lift your arms like a flight attendant and say, "If you are in line, you will fit between my arms." Quickly follow up with "If you are in line, the only thing you should be able to see is the back of a head." Anticipating that a child will try to cut in line someday, proactively work through this situation by teaching students exactly what to say: "Excuse me, please. I don't think you saw me standing here." The other child is taught to say, "Oh, excuse me, there you go." It may sound impossible, but it works. If it does not, try not to focus on the offender, as you may not be able to control him or her if he or she is in a defensive mode. Instead, suggest to the other child, "Wow. You were so polite and it didn't work? That's really too bad. I would just move away from that person." That is usually the way it would happen in the adult world. If not, there would some awful brawls in banks, grocery stores, and department stores.

- **How to form a circle.** Forming a circle is another perfect example of a nonacademic lesson that is quite necessary to allow for quick transitions for whole group discussion purposes. Teach children to approximate the size and go for it collectively. Anyone left out of the circle is taught to tap a peer and politely say, "Excuse me, please. Could you move back?"

    Practice forming circles again and again within the first week or two of school. You do not have to do anything major with them other than recognize what a great circle it is and comment on how it is important to move so efficiently and effectively. You may choose to do a read aloud or some other brief lesson at this point, but remember, your lesson objective is simply to help children learn how to make discussion circles quickly.

- **How to share or to ask someone to share with you.** Knowing that the teacher is eager to share the classroom with students, students are usually comfortable sharing. However, it is still important to teach them how to do so. The verbiage you provide is critical. "Katie, may I share that with you? I'd really like to" or "Michael, may I have that when you are finished?" Students have two choices for responses, "Yes, I will share" or "Not right now, but as soon as I am finished, I will give it to you." The latter may be accompanied with a reminder on a sticky note so that it is not forgotten, especially if you are running out of time. The best way to teach this is through modeling and role-playing with students. Be sure to make the verbiage for asking and responding to one another very specific, as part of the reason that sharing is such a challenge is that many children simply do not have the words to use. As always, reinforce appropriate sharing behavior with very specific feedback on what the child has done.

- **Whose turn it is to talk.** Raising hands to speak is a decent way to manage outbursts, but it can be quite overwhelming when there are twenty or so waving hands all partnered with "Oh, oh, oh!" or "Me, me, me!" A quick and easy way to turn this around is to invite children to put up only their thumb or pointer finger and to keep it right next to their shoulder instead of waving their entire arm madly in the air. An added benefit is that it allows you to see at a glance who is ready with the answer and who might benefit from additional support or direction.

> *It did not take me long to figure out that raising your hand (or finger) was not the only method I needed to use to help children in knowing whose turn it was to talk. As I began to investigate adult conversations, I noticed that individuals have conversations quite successfully without raising their hands—even in large groups. Have you ever been to a dinner party where the guests are required to raise their hand to speak? People know when to talk because they read one another's body language and watch their eyes. Children can learn how to do the same. Begin by explicitly teaching conversation skills to students. Teach students to watch your eyes as you ask a question. Then have them practice identifying who should answer your question as you stare right into one child's eyes while asking, "Who would I want to answer me now?" After a few demonstrations, children pick up pretty quickly, and the number of "shout-outs" diminishes rapidly. —Lisa*

- **How to listen to the loudspeaker.** The very first time the loudspeaker squawks, say, "Freeze!" and then stare up at the loudspeaker with the most intent expression on your face that you can possibly muster. Afterward, comment, "Is Mrs. Maloney here?" or "Do any of you own that car with its lights on?" or "Oh, yum! Hot dogs for lunch today!" In some way, react to the information, pointing out how important it is for everyone to listen closely. Pretty soon, every student will learn to do it along with you.

- **Teach "reverse tattling."** As most teachers do not want children to tattle, this is something that they would rather not address but find that they have to. With a large number of children together, all seeking attention, some students find this a successful way of monopolizing the teacher's time. Unfortunately, they also manage to alienate their peers at the same time (Everston, Emmer, and Worsham 2003). Tattlers are usually attention seekers or children who do not know how to handle the situation. Telling them to stop tattling is like telling Niagara Falls to stop flowing—it probably will not happen. Instead of creating a no tattling rule, teach your students how to do the exact opposite. In reverse tattling, students look for things to celebrate rather than things to complain about.

> *When I realized that my "No tattling!" rule was clearly not working, I opted to try something new and instituted what I have since labeled (but never to the children) as* reverse tattling. *In reverse tattling, I teach children to share only the great, wonderful, kind, and helpful things others do. It took a bit of time, but it certainly paid off. After spending several weeks of sharing sessions focusing on "Is there anyone out there who can tell me about something nice that someone did for them today?" I started to feel that my students had caught on. Tattling was dramatically reduced, but I knew for sure that reverse tattling had caught on the day I found myself standing on the playground with my new principal, after working on reverse tattling for about a month. As we stood there, a student came peeling across the playground, heading straight for me, mad as a hornet. Inwardly, I cringed, worried about what was to come out, knowing full well that my new boss was certainly watching with a close eye. As the student finally caught his breath, he blurted out, "Ms. D! Ms. D! I can't believe this! I was just knocked down and only three kids came to help me up!" The "no tattling" rule failed; however, my reverse tattling expectation was an overwhelming success. Even though the student was tattling, his focus was not on the student who knocked him down; it was on the fact that only three of nineteen students came to help him up. If the biggest complaint I get is from a child who was concerned that only three of his friends, and not all nineteen, had come to his rescue, I'll consider my "reverse tattling" efforts a victory. —Lisa*

- **Learning silent signals.** You may find it useful to teach your students some simple sign language that can be used as silent signals in the classroom. Teachers tend to repeat explicit directions like "Sit down" or "Be quiet" over and over again. Behavior that requires repeated addressing such as this is an indication that student self-managing behaviors need to be revisited, but at times, students just need a gentle reminder or redirection, for example during assemblies when the teacher would prefer not to interact verbally with her students, but needs to prompt self-managing behavior.

  Create simple signs for such things as "Sit down" or "Be quiet" so that you can address behavior quickly, but without taking attention away from the task at hand. Also, if a student is required to ask before leaving for the bathroom, that child can make the pre-determined sign for "toilet," allowing the teacher to continue the lesson without stopping and answering, but instead giving permission through another signal, a nod, or shake of the head. Additional useful signs include pay attention, yes, no, stand up, lower your voice, and clean up, as well as many more that you may find valuable.

Section 2

Working Outside of the Classroom

It is important that teachers realize that their responsibilities extend beyond the walls of the classroom. How students act outside your classroom is in part a reflection of you and your teaching. Therefore, it is in your best interest to take time to support students to function effectively outside the classroom as well as within it.

- **How to walk in the hallway.** It is wise to always preteach how to walk in the hallway. If you do not, you will end up trying to teach students while running late for art class and end up just racing them through the hallway. Plan about five minutes every once in a while at the beginning of the year to practice walking respectfully in the hallway. You may want to teach this after your how-to-form-a-line lesson. Then all you have to teach students is which side of the hall to walk on, how to keep their hands off the walls, and how to stop at every hallway or stairwell so that the end of the line can catch up. After students have learned how to do this successfully, place yourself at the end of the line, not at the beginning. That way, you can watch everything that is happening.

> *I do not believe that having children march through the hallway with their finger over their lips is beneficial, as I have never walked down a hallway that way as an adult. I remind my children daily that being quiet in the hallway is important because other children are trying to learn, and they respect that.* —Lisa

> *I wonder why I never learned how to walk a class down the hallway during my teacher training in college. Seems odd to think that this could be a big deal, but it was. It took me only a few days to realize that leading my line down the hallway did not allow me to observe student interaction. When I realized the importance of having eyes in the back of my head, I repositioned myself at the end of my line. A student became the line leader with the responsibility of choosing where to stop along our route to keep everyone together. The line leaders loved the leadership opportunity given to them, and I had the perfect position for observing student behavior. A win-win!* —Amy Goodman; Middle School Literacy Teacher; Anchorage, Alaska

- **How to behave in the lunchroom.** Once students are in the lunchroom, you may be officially off duty and not responsible for their behavior; however, as mentioned earlier, the way students behave outside of your immediate presence is in part a reflection of you and your teaching. To this end, spend time teaching children how to sit and behave properly—regardless of what they see other children doing. One important thing you can teach them to do is determine whom they should and should not choose to talk with at their table. Part of the reason it gets so loud in the lunchroom is that children are talking to their friends sitting ten feet away. Teach children to talk with the people next to them

Chapter 4: Establishing Ongoing Routines

and the person across from them, and not the kid at the end of the table. It is wise to spend some time at the beginning of the year in the lunchroom when no one else is there and role-play what the lunch hour should be like. It is important again to teach them appropriate language to use. If someone is speaking to them in a voice that is too loud or from too far away, children need to be prepared to say, "Can you please speak more quietly? I am sitting right next to you" or "Wait until we're finished with lunch, please. I'll see you on the playground."

> *In an attempt at community service, I ask my students to say something nice to the cafeteria workers every day such as "Thank you for the peas" or "Your new pin is really pretty." Whatever they want, just something nice. I can hardly walk past the lunchroom door without cringing at the chaos the workers deal with for hours every day. They deserve some additional kindness and appreciation. —Lisa*

> *In an attempt to allow students and staff to know each other better, I invite custodians, resource teachers, the principal, and the cafeteria workers to come to our classroom every other Friday afternoon to join us for "Family Fridays." During "Family Fridays," visitors, who also include family members, siblings, and sometimes older book buddies, enter our room, kick off their shoes, and treat our classroom like a living room. Each adult (or book buddy) sits with one or more of my students and reads with them. Soon, meaningful relationships form, connecting the random adults (staff members) to our students. My students seem more likely to respect the adults, and vice versa, in our building once the relationship is there. —Sarah*

- **How to behave on the bus.** Whether on a field trip or on their way home, students' behavior is again a reflection of their teacher. Take time to teach your children how to get on and off the bus, as well as how to behave while on it. Students should know that the only people they should talk to on the bus are the people next to or across from them and possibly the children sitting on the aisle in front of or behind them. Speak to them earnestly about what a great responsibility the driver has for the safety of each passenger.

> *Most bus companies offer this service with the yearly bus evacuation drill, but I find that reviewing this information is extremely beneficial. I even teach my students to say something nice to the driver before departing. Every year, I ask one of the drivers to come a little early or stay a little late so that I can take the time to do this—I have never been refused. In fact, my efforts have been so successful, not only do my students receive compliments regularly, one time I received a marriage proposal! —Lisa*

Section 2

Instruction

Teachers can share specific strategies with students to ensure that they are successful learners. The ongoing routines are geared largely toward making teaching and learning possible. The routines in this section are more specifically linked to enhancing the learning potential for each individual student.

- **How to listen.** This is similar to how to listen to the loudspeaker (see Teaching Routines); however, here the emphasis is on students listening to the teacher or to each other with their eyes and ears. Spend time showing children how to face the speaker to watch his or her eyes and mouth movements. People who appear to lack social skills may often just lack the ability to infer from other people's words and voices. This is something you can easily help children do through role-playing and practice. Ask children to watch you as you listen to someone (for example, when the principal or another teacher comes in) and then, afterward, ask them to identify what you did. They will point out that you kept your eyes on the visitor, nodded your head, repeated parts of what they said, and asked questions if you did not understand. Without instruction or focusing their attention on this, children may not ever learn how to listen.

- **How to think.** Some children do not know how to process information effectively. This is another one of those tasks that remains invisible to children as it is buried so deeply within their minds. The best way to bring this out is to start to "think aloud" for your children, making your behaviors explicit. You may encourage students to watch how you stare up toward the ceiling as you think aloud to yourself (Keene and Zimmerman 1997).

> *I usually show students how I stare at the ceiling, scrunch up my forehead, tap my chin or temple, and share what I am thinking. "Let's see, what do I think is going to happen next? Well, I can see that this man is going really fast because of the motion lines. And I can see this man walking with a giant birthday cake. If the first man keeps on going, he might crash into the other one when he gets to the corner. Oh! If they crash, the birthday cake would get ruined!"*
> —Lisa

Chapter 4: Establishing Ongoing Routines

Assessment

Assessment is not something children need to learn a routine for; they just need to understand that it is something you do to learn about your students. Be very clear and positive with students, identifying what you are doing and why so that assessment is not a mystery or something to fear (Clay 1993). As you take a running record, you can say, "I'm just going to listen to you read so I can learn about the strategies you use. After I listen to you read, I will know exactly what I need to teach you so that you can be an even better reader." Through such positive interactions, children will learn that assessment is not something to be feared and that it only takes a brief amount of time and then they can get right back to work.

> ### Efficiency and Effectiveness Task
>
> ### Overcoming Trouble Spots
>
> Return to the list you wrote at the beginning of the chapter. Determine a routine that can be instituted that will render your "trouble spots" obsolete. Using the Teaching Routines Checklist in the appendix, record the specific routines that you will use in each of the categories listed and record those in your lesson plan book, identifying exactly when you will introduce each of these routines, just as you would an instructional academic lesson.

Teaching Routines Checklist

	Routines	Date introduced	Dates Revisited
Using materials			
Managing noise levels			
Getting help			
Getting students' attention			
Working inside the classroom (alone and with others)			
Working outside the classroom			

Chapter 5

Putting It All Together for the First Weeks of School

> A sense of community begins during the earliest days of the school year, but wise teachers in the upper elementary grades find lots of ways to foster it throughout the year. (Calkins 1986, 146)

Harry Wong (1998) is relentless in his reminders that teachers must dedicate a significant amount of time during the beginning of the school year to establish a solid foundation upon which to build throughout the year. Chapter 4 looked closely at the ongoing routines that teachers should introduce and revisit. The time schedule for these routines is dependent on you and your students, but you must address all of them directly and repeatedly if you intend for students to integrate them into their repertoire of behaviors. This chapter provides a more focused view of what certain time frames leading up to the sixth week of school might include.

Before School Starts

Before school starts, try to get rid of everything you have not used for a year or so to clear your classroom of clutter. Children often become overwhelmed and distracted in an over-stimulating environment that offers too many choices and is unorganized (Bickart, Jablon, and Dodge 1999). It is in your best interest to do a massive spring-cleaning every summer (refer to section 1 for more information on organizing your classroom).

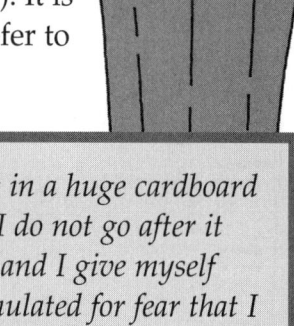

If I am afraid to pitch it because I think I might need it again, I put it in a huge cardboard box and keep it for a year, using it as a table or shelf of some sort. If I do not go after it during that year, I know that I probably will not go after it ever again, and I give myself permission to pitch it. It is hard to let go of materials that I have accumulated for fear that I may need them sometime in the future, but there is a limit to what I can keep holding onto.
—Lisa

At the beginning of every school year, my classroom is one of the most popular ones for other teachers to visit. That's because it's a well-known fact that I begin every school year getting rid of as much as I possibly can. Outside of my classroom, I set a table. As I sort through all of my belongings, I place on the table anything that I no longer want, need, or use. My colleagues know that they can stroll by and take anything they like, and we all benefit. They have something useful, and I have more room! —Sarah

Try to start the school year with your classroom virtually barren and without a stitch on the walls. A classroom that is "decorated" at the beginning of the year does little to nothing to enhance the learning of the students or the building of a community. The classroom should grow and develop as the students within it do, so as the year goes on and resources are needed, pull them out of your storage system.

There are other physical concerns you will need to address before school starts. Revisit chapter 1 as you work to establish the geography for your room and consider placement of furniture and other organizational systems you are putting into place. Also consider your resources. Do you have enough books or materials? If not, what are you going to do about it? You might consider creating a "wish list" to share with parents. You could also create a bulletin board featuring a giant Giving Tree, a la Shel Silverstein (1964), with removable apples that each have a needed item recorded on the surface for parents to pull. You could even research and write a grant for money to purchase items that you need. Millions of dollars of grant money go unclaimed every year—take advantage of this.

The week or so before school starts, take the opportunity to send a note to your students on brightly colored paper, saying something to the effect of "I can't wait to meet you! On the first day of school I'll be wearing... Look for me on the playground. Bring your favorite book to school that day." You might consider including a brightly colored pen or pencil in the envelope as well. For some students, this may be the only letter they have ever received in their life. This may also be the only piece of property they can truly call their own. This is a small investment in building a relationship with students that is well worth the amount of money it costs.

Before school starts is also a time to think carefully about what you expect this year to bring for you. Review your curriculum, the report card, and any checklists or scope and sequences you can get your hands on so that you can build a continuum in your head for where it is that you are hoping to bring your students. Once you have laid that continuum down in your mind, it is time to meet your children so that you can begin to learn where they fall on that continuum. The rest of the year will then be dedicated to supporting each individual child as he or she makes progress.

The First Day of School

One of the most important things you can do on the first day of school is to establish the understanding in your students that this is an enjoyable place of order where learning will occur, and, although you are clearly in charge, it is a place where everyone will share. Keeping this in mind, try to keep academics on the first day to the bare minimum. You have approximately 179 academic calendar days left, and it is more important to set the tone that will carry you through those days than to try to fill students' heads with knowledge the second they walk in the door.

Most of the first day should be dedicated to learning about one another and how the class is going to function for the rest of the year and enjoying great literature. Also teach

Section 2

general routines, such as how to sit, where to sit, and how to talk to each other. Most importantly, stress that the classroom is a community in which every student is an active and welcome member. Refer to the ongoing routines in chapter 4 and use the strategies as a menu to pull from for your lesson plans. Choose the activities that will be of greatest benefit to you in establishing the kind of environment that will allow you and your students to experience success. "The idea is to provide students with the information they need to complete successfully the activities required of them in the first days of school and to help them feel confident in their new classroom environment" (Evertson, Emmer, and Worsham 2003, 66).

> Effective teachers introduce rules, procedures, and routines on the very first day of school and continue to teach them the first week of school....The ineffective teacher is too eager to present lessons; consequently, when misbehavior occurs, they discipline—often without a plan. (Wong 1998, 141)

Balance the more formal instruction with ongoing read alouds and introductions to big books, poems, and songs throughout the day. Remember that these children may have spent the summer break running around on their own personal clocks. Take care to pay attention to their attention span and try to work well within its limits. The attention span for focused, direct instruction is roughly equal to a student's age in minutes, but expect it to be even less than that on the first day of school (Jensen 1995). The goal is to send children home at the end of the day knowing that this is a serious place of learning as well as one that they will want to return to daily.

> *I watch my children like a hawk that first day, jotting down dozens of mental notes that I will pour onto paper at the end of the day. This task is made easier by connecting children's names to the faces in the pictures I took that day with either a digital or self-developing camera. At the end of the day, I sit down at a table and spread out all of the pictures of the students, matching notes I took throughout the day to their faces at the same time additional thoughts come to mind as my memory is jogged by looking at the pictures.* —Lisa

You also might want to collect a writing sample on the first day of school. Knowing that assessment drives effective instruction, it makes sense to collect as much initial data and information as possible to ensure that your initial instruction and expectations meet the needs and abilities of your students. Make sure to begin every sample with a modeled writing lesson, after which you can ask the children to write for you. If you pose the task correctly, this should not be a challenging or frustrating first day activity. Take care not to ask the students to do something challenging that could have lasting, negative repercussions throughout the year. Here are some examples of what you might do:

Chapter 5: Putting It All Together for the First Weeks of School

- **Provide a text that students can respond to directly.** For example, "Dear Class, I am so happy to be at school today. When I am not in school I like to... What do you like to do? Love, Ms. ..." Having children respond to this letter allows you to get to know them personally, as well as provides some insight into their strengths and needs as writers. Was this stressful? Were they creative? What sort of letter-sound mapping do you see evidence of?

- **Write a letter that would also double as a launch for your writing station.** For example, "Dear Class, Fourth grade is going to be great! I am going to work hard to... Do you have any other advice for me? What can I do to make this year great for you? Love, Ms. ..." Think of how much you could learn about children's character as well as their current status as writers.

All of the data you collect through these interactions becomes the initial foundation for your upcoming instruction. The writing samples also become the first that you may continue to collect on the first school day of every month from this day forward.

This day has been critical in setting the tone for the rest of your time together. The children have told you loud and clear what they know and can do, and you have an idea about what you would like for them to learn next.

The First Week of School

After learning about your children on the first day of school, you are closer to exploring academic instructional opportunities; however, you must continue to put the greatest emphasis on establishing the classroom culture that will carry you for the rest of the year. "Student achievement at the end of the year is directly related to the degree to which the teacher establishes good control of the classroom procedures in the very first week of school" (Wong 1998, 4). The remainder of the first week of school, therefore, is largely dedicated to more fact-finding and establishing guidelines and routines.

> *During the first week of school, my students and I discuss expectations. My students do most of the talking, while I ask questions that facilitate our discussion. By the end of the week, I ask them to work with their table groups to come up with their expectations for different segments of our day, for example, independent writing time or recess. After a set time, the chart is passed to another group that reads the list and adds their thoughts. Each group is responsible for writing at least one expectation. After gathering all of the students' ideas, we work as an entire class to compose a final list. We always record each expectation in a positive and specific manner. For example, "Remember that other students are trying to learn. If you have to talk in the hallway, please whisper!" instead of "Be respectful of others in the hallway" or "Don't talk in the hallway." —Sarah*

Section 2

"As the teacher you certainly have the power to lay down the ground rules, but the more you base these rules on needs as they arise and involve the children in reasoning out why specific rules would be helpful to all of them, the more likely those rules are to be followed" (Forester and Reinhard 1994, 160). Provide instruction at your students' point of need, whether it be in the academic or behavioral realm. Children are able to take on new learning if instruction is provided at the right time and place (Vygotsky 1962). Reflect on the following:

- **How did this go?**
- **Is there a way it could have gone better?**
- **What advice do you have for other students who will try this tomorrow?**

Toward the end of the first week, slowly begin to introduce independent work activities. Begin with the most simplistic one—independent reading in the class library. Do not assume that your students already know how to use all the materials in your classroom. Make sure to introduce everything in your classroom: where it is and how to use it (Bickart, Jablon, and Dodge 1999).

Once you and your students are confident that an activity can be moved to the independent level, start with a small group of children. For example, have four or five children go off to read independently, while you work with the rest of the group on some sort of whole group reading or writing task. The goal of independent work at this point is not to challenge children academically; rather, the goal is to pour their energy into establishing independent work behaviors. Make sure to choose simple tasks that they can easily experience success with. That way, all of their efforts can be dedicated to making good decisions about working independently. "Planning activities that will allow all of your students to be successful will make students feel more secure and confident and will encourage their continued good effort" (Evertson, Emmer, and Worsham 2003, 62).

> *I introduce many of my independent work activities through a fishbowl format wherein a small group of children sits in the center of a circle performing an activity while the rest of us look on and observe. Afterward, we share with one another what we saw, acknowledging appropriate and inappropriate behaviors. When things run smoothly, we acknowledge the behaviors in concrete terms. When we discover something that did not go well, we work as a group to determine an amenable solution. —Lisa*

After spending the first few days doing modeled and shared writing lessons, introduce personal writing notebooks. Writing notebooks are more general than journals, which are often used more like diaries. Everything students write can go into these notebooks. You might provide the notebooks, or consider allowing students to get their own—that way they are more personalized (Hindley 1996).

Chapter 5: Putting It All Together for the First Weeks of School

At the beginning of the year, work to introduce a number of different writing genres and text types: lists, labels, letters, personal narrative stories, magazine picture stories, poetry, and factual text on single topics or comparing more than one. As time goes on, students will have a pretty healthy list of forms they can choose from for their writing practice that day. If children are complaining or struggling with the fact that they "don't know what to write about," do not assume you need to provide them with a prompt. You may have asked them to do too much too soon. If this occurs, provide mini-lessons and model how to come up with an idea of what to write about.

Start to pepper the walls of the classroom with the texts generated from whole-group writing lessons. The print is purposeful and meaningful because it was created for, with, or by your students. Avoid "decorating" your classroom; instead, develop a print-rich environment over time (see chapter 1 for more information on how to set up the classroom). "How you set up the room will convey powerful messages to the children. There is no need to spend a lot of money or time on lavish bulletin board displays. A sparsely decorated room with lots of empty wall space conveys the message 'This is our classroom, and we will decide together how to decorate it'" (Bickart, Jablon, and Dodge 1999, 52).

> *The first year I taught, I modeled writing every day during the first week of school and made the mistake of never doing so again. It is almost embarrassing to think back to that first year when I can quote myself in April saying "Sure, you know how to do that. Don't you remember when I showed you how to do it in September?" It took me far too long, but I finally realized that writing in front of or providing a writing mini-lesson for children is something that needs to be done on a regular basis as they are constantly learning new and different things about writing and need ongoing support. —Lisa*

As a welcome to the classroom, honor students by publishing their names around the room over the next week. To honor and recognize students as important members of the classroom community, write each of their names in bubble letters as large as a foot and a half high, with each letter darkly outlined so that they can be clearly seen from across the room. Have students decorate each letter in a manner that represents themselves. For example, a student who loves sports may decorate each letter with pictures of baseballs or other sports paraphernalia. A student who has a passion for animals may cut pictures of animals from a magazine and add them to his or her visual display. (You may choose to have children make their own bubble letters to increase their ownership and involvement, but, in this case, we do not encourage that. The names will be published on the wall and referred to throughout the year and their clear visibility is important. Some children may not draw the lines boldly enough to make the words useful and others may be frustrated by the task altogether—neither of which would be conducive to the construction of this powerful resource. There are plenty of opportunities for children to take on a higher degree of ownership; this may not be one of them.)

As they are completed, review the names with students by exploring the letters, sounds,

> Your name is very important. It identifies and dignifies you. Other people in the world may have the same letters as your name, but as far as you are concerned, you are the only person in the world with your name. It is a name that you can easily hear above the din of a crowd. And when you hear your name, you pay attention.... You pay attention because you are important! (Wong 1998, 70)

and phonetic combinations—all the aspects that make that word unique. Have students explain the decisions they made as they created their piece, sharing important insights into themselves, and then let the students choose where they want to hang their names. Continue to refer to their names in the same way you use the Word Wall—the students' names become anchors and resources for spelling and writing.

Along with writing instruction, begin reading instruction. Daily, provide quality read alouds and exposure to enlarged texts that you can explore with your students, establishing a core of old favorites and learning together to love reading and writing.

As far as collecting assessment data, record students' general attitudes and abilities related to reading and writing. Continue to review their writing efforts as they record things in their notebooks, all the while reflecting, "What is it that they need to learn right now?"

As you introduce independent work activities, find time to start to listen to children read. Try to sit separately with at least four different children each day, listening to each one read. Provide a range of texts and ask students to choose their own to see what they perceive themselves capable of doing. It is helpful to keep a set of leveled books on hand so that you can begin to benchmark students in comparison to one another. Take informal reading records, jotting down notes on each child as you listen to him or her read. As you observe their behaviors, look for comprehension, finger pointing, fluency, pauses, hesitations, skipping words, sounding out, and so on. Basically, take note of any behavior children engage in to help you build a growing profile of who each child is as a reader. This is also a good time to begin filling in checklists and having students complete self-assessments and interest surveys.

End every day during this week, and for the rest of the year for that matter, asking students to reflect, "What did we learn today about reading and writing, and what did we learn about each other? What did we learn about working together?" These daily updates and conversations will support decision-making processes for the rest of the year.

Week Two

Vygotsky's assertion that "what the child can do in cooperation today he can do alone tomorrow" (1962, 104) neatly parallels the gradual release of responsibility theory, which is the foundation of a comprehensive literacy program. It is important to support students as they learn to take responsibility for their behavior and as they establish independent work behaviors. Not only will this reduce daily stress related to ongoing management issues, but it will also provide you with the time and freedom to work with small groups of students, knowing that the rest of the class is capable of working on their own for an extended period of time.

Chapter 5: Putting It All Together for the First Weeks of School

The first week of school was dedicated to introductions and explorations of different independent tasks. Spend the next two weeks gradually introducing more options and longer time spans dedicated to independent work. The progression of this will depend entirely on who you are, who your students are, and what you hope to accomplish.

Assuming that students were successful in their endeavors in week one, move to sending two groups off to read independently while you continue to work with the rest of the class. Slightly increase the time frames from five minutes to eight or ten or increase the number of students working independently. Continue playing with all of these numbers, working aggressively to have more students working successfully for longer periods of time. As long as students continue to demonstrate success, continue to push the boundaries gently. Begin by increasing the amount of time children are working independently, or increase the number of students working independently, or increase the number of choices available to them. Do not do all three at once—chaos will surely ensue, and it is quite difficult for students to "unlearn" undesirable habits.

Soon, your students will be ready for you to introduce additional activities as well as the classroom library. You may want to start with a listening station, as it is quite simplistic. Then move on to an art station, and finally move to other learning stations or other independent work opportunities when you feel that your students are ready to take on more options. Take great care to ensure that you are not offering or asking too much too soon. It is always easy to add more choices, but it is extremely difficult to backtrack and take choices away from students or to extinguish bad habits that are formed when you move too quickly. Although you want children to settle into independent work patterns, remember that time spent wisely at the beginning of the year is truly an investment that will most certainly pay off in the long run.

As you continue working to establish proper independent work behaviors, the amount and quality of your reflective time with students increases proportionately. Use the following questions to reflect on with your students:

- **What worked today? What did not?**
- **What will you do tomorrow so that you do not have that problem again?**
- **What advice do you have for others who will work in that area tomorrow?**
- **Did you have a classmate help you in any way today? Tell me about it.**
- **Was anyone especially kind to you? Tell me about it.**

Regular class meetings are critical in fostering responsible student behavior. If you believe students can behave responsibly, and you support them properly and invest the time, they will not disappoint you. If you believe they will struggle or fail, they will.

The thrust of the second week can be summarized as an exploration of choices and children. There is an increase in the academic instruction at this point, but it is a gradual one as you work hard to learn about your students at the same time. The text that you jointly generate through modeled and shared writing lessons begins to fill the room with engaging and meaningful print. The children work to develop and embrace their classroom home as you simultaneously work to assist in their development and embrace them as learners.

Every step your students take toward more independent work behaviors allows you greater opportunities to learn more about them as you engage in ongoing formal and informal assessments (see chapter 3 for more information on managing formal and informal assessments). Reading observations and other pencil-paper assessments are a breeze now, as you have small windows of time throughout the day to devote to assessment purposes.

These first weeks may be some of the most exhausting of the school year as you find yourself "fishing" with students: Cast them out and let them go a little way; then reel them back in for a quick check, before casting them out once again. This "letting go" and then "pulling back" continues for the rest of the school year as you continue to release them a little further and for a bit longer every time, according to the gradual release of responsibility model.

Week Three

At this point, you may find yourself getting a bit antsy. You have introduced your students to a wide range of activities, the majority of your instruction has been in a whole group format, and you may be itching to start organizing and working with small groups. It is important to remember that although you may be ready or feel the pressure to move on, your students may not be ready. It is easy to move ahead too quickly, but you run the risk of assisting your students in learning inappropriate behaviors that may be very hard to extinguish or redirect. The independent work activities found in section 3 serve as a collection of tasks that students can engage in during the time you spend pulling students to work in small groups. The amount of choice and freedom you offer will be different every year, depending on your group of students.

Throughout this window of time, continue releasing responsibility for independent work efforts. More children should be working independently with more choices available to them. You have most likely done enough whole group reading and writing work that you can offer independent activities, such as a writing station, a working with words station, or a listening station, in addition to your classroom library (see section 3 for more details on these stations). You can establish each independent work option and continue to add more throughout the year as the children develop in their proficiency as readers and writers.

When you feel the time is right, introduce the work board or whatever more formal management structure you have decided to use (see section 3 for more information on work boards). As students are learning to understand the stations, ensure that the tasks are manageable. For example, the first week you have a work board up, you might only have one, maybe two, activities that you expect students to move through—the most simplistic activities you can find. The goal is for students to learn how to work successfully within this new set of structures, not to be challenged by an activity within them.

> When introducing the work board, I choose to make the tasks easier so that more of students' energy can be focused on aligning themselves to the structure I am asking them to function within. I generally start with only one group on the work board at a time, and keep the rest with me. If I decide to start with all children working independently, four out of the five groups are probably working on the same activity—usually book boxes, or something simple. —Lisa

The next week, you can add another layer to the work board, extend the choices, or lengthen the work time, but not all three at once. Increase the degree of challenge the tasks pose only after children have demonstrated that they are capable of working within the boundaries of the system you have put in place. Once this system has had its kinks worked out (through time, dialogue, and problem-solving with the students), you are ready to pull your small reading groups together.

It may take up to week four or beyond to get things up and running to this degree. Until then, most of your instructional time continues to be dedicated to whole group activities and assessment. Whole group writing leads to significant amounts of print being added to the walls, and reading strategies continue to be unveiled through the daily read-aloud and shared-reading sessions.

Assessments from weeks one and two, as well as any other assessment systems you have put into place (see chapter 3), allow you to begin to formulate groups that you will start to pull soon. In organizing for small group reading instruction, first divide a piece of paper into boxes. Label each box with a developmental reading stage. Depending on the grade level and population, label the boxes with the following terms (see chapter 3 for more information):

- **Pre-emergent**
- **Emergent** (You might even break this down into Emergent 1, 2, and 3 or Pre-emergent/Emergent and Emergent/Early.)
- **Early** (You can break this down in the same fashion as the Emergent level.)
- **Early Fluent or Transitional**
- **Fluent** (You can break this down by more specific needs. For example, you may organize a group to support students who have an over-reliance on phonics or a group of students who read fluently but do not comprehend what they are reading.)

After organizing this informal classroom reading profile, note the month on the top of the sheet and place your students' names in the chart to the best of your ability (repeat this at the onset of every month during the school year as a record of class and individual progress). Before week four and on an ongoing basis, fine-tune your estimates.

Week Four and Beyond

Finally, you arrive at week four (or week five or six, depending on your particular situation this year). At this point, you can begin to pull together small groups for reading instruction. Prior to doing so, be sure you are fully confident that your students are capable of working independently. You will know that you have reached that point in developing independent work behaviors when you can stand back in your classroom and watch your children functioning smoothly without you.

As you begin pulling together reading groups, start with only one a day and slowly work up to two or three. If you find that students are unable to work independently for an extended period of time, break up a longer independent work time into shorter segments of time, punctuated with whole group reading or writing opportunities. For example, instead of expecting your students to work independently for forty minutes, ask them to work for two smaller blocks of twenty minutes each, with a shared-reading lesson or some other whole group learning opportunity sandwiched in between each of the independent work/small group reading instruction blocks.

Continue to collect both formal and informal information on your students every day for the rest of the year. These assessments are invaluable in letting you know what to teach from day to day.

If you have worked hard to establish an environment characterized by order, you can fully expect that everything will run smoothly the vast majority of the time; however, every now and then children will slip. It would be a mistake to gather children only when troubles arise—it is often too late by that point and some bad habits have been learned. Alternately, it is wise to take time on a regular basis to celebrate the successes and to identify and articulate the behaviors and decisions that are good ones, so they will be honored and repeated. Taking a few steps back to recognize and reinforce (and possibly reteach) acceptable behavior is something that will continue to occur throughout the school year. It is extremely helpful to recognize this and plan for it.

> The most important thing these teachers do is that often throughout the year they call youngsters together to talk about the issues of their lives. If a few children taunt another child, these teachers are not apt to pull the offenders into the hall for a brief lecture and then carry on with the curriculum. Instead, the entire class gathers together. The room is filled with an air of great seriousness. (Calkins 1987, 146–7)

Handling Challenging Behavior

There is no doubt that effective teaching must begin with effective classroom management. A classroom ruled by chaos or constant behavioral problems is one that is not conducive to teaching or learning successfully. The solid foundation that appropriate classroom management provides will greatly diminish the possibility of both overall chaos and potential behavioral problems (Routman 2000, 161).

Establishing a truly well-managed classroom requires a great deal of time, effort, and patience on the part of the teacher. It usually requires considerable amounts of trial and error as well (Routman 2000). The bulk of this text has been dedicated to coordinating routines and structures that will allow both the teacher and students to function successfully as a community, in essence, a well-managed classroom.

Such proactive measures are desirable, but teachers must address the fact that effective teaching is not fail-safe. No matter how well you set up the classroom, your instruction, and the routines and procedures that are the foundation of your classroom, from time to time, students will act out.

The position you take in responding to and handling behavior problems is a direct reflection of your beliefs. If you believe that you are the ruler of the classroom and that order and control flow from you, you might expect to have a long and tiresome year. The control of students comes from within themselves. You can set up the parameters within which they can function and establish routines and guidelines along with them, but the ultimate choices children make are up to them. Losing your temper and responding by yelling or threatening will only escalate undesirable behavior, or result in students shutting down as a result of the threats.

> Learning cannot occur in an environment where student behavior is out of control. If students are running around, defying the teacher, or picking fights, they cannot also engage deeply with content. Of course, the reverse is also true: When students are engaged deeply with content, they are less likely to pick fights, defy a teacher, or run around a classroom. (Danielson 1996, 85)

Avoiding Rewards and Punishment

A focus on the teacher's needs being met through coercion and bribery or rewards and punishment may have an immediate positive outcome, but this type of management may have long-term negative consequences. Such responses sometimes result in immediate success, but that success is usually followed with a quick return to the original behavior. Such methods for changing behavior are very teacher centered and do not address the learners' behavior in a way that will bring about lasting change. Effective teachers take time to help students reflect on their behavior and assume the responsibility for and control of their own actions (Kohn 1993). "To help students become ethical people, as opposed to people who merely do what they are told, we cannot merely tell them what to do. We have to help them figure out—for themselves and with each other—how one ought to act. That's why dropping the tools of traditional discipline, like rewards and consequences, is only the beginning. It's even more crucial that we overcome a preoccupation with getting compliance and instead involve students in devising and justifying ethical principles" (Kohn 1998, 15).

Extending and removing privileges such as recess time, tickets, or points to be exchanged for prizes, stickers, and so on are also not effective in supporting students to alter their behavior. A more logical approach would be to focus on the needs of the student and the behavior itself. Instead of removing a choice or a student, it is important to take the time to address the problem such that the solution is not merely a temporary one but a long-lasting one. Focus your efforts consistently toward coordinating "ongoing structures that will support today's and tomorrow's work, rather than planning one time arrangements" (Calkins 1999, 14).

> If your objective is to get people to obey an order, to show up on time and do what they're told, then bribing or threatening them may be sensible strategies. But if your objective is to get long-term quality in the workplace, to help students become careful thinkers and self-directed learners, or to support children in developing good values, then rewards, like punishments, are absolutely useless. In fact, as we are beginning to see, they are worse than useless—they are actually counterproductive. (Kohn 1993, 41)

Focusing on the Behavior, Not the Child

The most appropriate response to undesirable behavior is that which results in minimal disruption to the classroom rhythm and focuses on the behavior, not the child (Danielson 1996). If you look to behavior problems as potential teaching points, a great deal of stress and pressure can be removed from the situation.

If there is a problem in the classroom, look at several components of the problem:

- **What was the problem?**
- **Whom does this problem affect?**
- **What was the underlying reason for the problem?**
- **How can we work to make sure that this does not take place again?**
- **What will we do next time?**

In responding to a behavioral problem, it is wise to view the situation as you would an academic one—as a teachable moment. If you look at behavioral problems as something to be solved and worked out together, the results will be markedly different than if the child were simply punished for the inappropriate behavior. Such a response is far more respectful of the learner and will be of greater benefit in the long run (Kohn 1993). Using the questions listed above, you will be able to address the situation more appropriately, rather than simply reacting to the student.

Chapter 5: Putting It All Together for the First Weeks of School

> When I was student teaching, my mentor, Reg, had a student in her class whom I will call Johnny. This student often acted out. I remember him doing something so awful one day that I fully expected Reg to go over and really yell at him. Instead, she walked up, hugged him, rocking back and forth saying, "Oh, Johnny, c'mon buddy. You know better than that. What could you have done here instead?" I was forever changed—as I am sure Johnny was as well. —Lisa

In his studies on how instructional management affects student behavior, Jacob Kounin (in Charles 1998) found that there is no relationship between what he calls teachers' desist techniques (remarks and reprimands to stop misbehavior) and the degree of success in handling unacceptable behavior. Instead of focusing on unsuccessful, negative attempts to manage or control the environment, Kounin focused his energy on identifying and nurturing positive strategies. These strategies include the following:

- **Withitness:** A high level of teacher awareness as to what is happening within all parts of the classroom at all times

- **Momentum and Smoothness:** Maintaining steady pace in instruction and activities, with comfortable and appropriate closure—transitions are smooth, seamless, and logical

- **Group Alerting and Accountability:** The ability to get students' attention quickly and providing directions or support succinctly—students are actively involved and engaged

- **Overlapping:** Teachers are capable of attending to more than one element of instruction at a time—teachers are in effect multi-tasking their instructional and behavior management efforts

- **Satiation and Challenge Arousal:** "Overload" results in satiation, which results directly in misbehavior, boredom, or other undesirable behaviors—a stimulating and challenging environment decreases the possibility of satiation

It is human nature to want to belong, to fit in, and to be successful. This is an innate need that all humans work to fulfill. When this primary goal is not met, behavior problems surface. A child will work to have his or her need to feel significant met, and if he is unable to do so successfully in a positive manner, he may revert to undesirable behavior (Walton and Powers 1974).

Rudolf Dreikurs (in Walton and Powers 1974) supports the belief that all behavior (whether positive or negative) is goal driven. He has narrowed down the mistaken goals of misbehavior into four categories: attention, power, revenge, or inadequacy. In observing misbehavior, an effective teacher is able to identify the mistaken goal and act accordingly.

> **Goal #1: ATTENTION** Students who do not feel a sense of belonging will act out in an effort to gain the attention of their teacher and peers. Students seeking attention will act out, make noises, provide distractions to teaching and learning, and other similar behaviors geared toward gaining the attention of others.
>
> **Goal #2: POWER** If they are not feeling that they are getting the attention they seek, some students will attempt to assert power or control over their situation. Such students may refuse to do work, defy authority, try to take over and do things their own way, disobey, lie, and may cry when they cannot have things their way.
>
> **Goal #3: REVENGE** Students who do not feel that they are getting attention and have lost their struggle for power may attempt to exact revenge on their teachers or others. These students demonstrate physical violence and/or verbal abuse of peers and adults.
>
> **Goal #4: INADEQUACY** When all other attempts at fulfilling their needs have failed, children protect themselves by withdrawing and refusing to participate in class activities.

Effective teachers identify the mistaken goal and respond by helping the child to understand the goal his or her misbehavior represents and identify a better strategy to lead to success. It is imperative that the teacher not make the behavior worthwhile to the child by offering attention for inappropriate behavior, engaging in a power struggle, supporting a need to exact revenge, or setting the child up to feel continued inadequacy.

By working with the child or the whole group in a class meeting or a conference, you can begin to explore the roots of the behavior and identify more acceptable alternative responses. If the class meetings referenced in section 1 have been taking place on a regular basis, children will be very

comfortable exploring more sensitive issues than the standard ones you focused on in the initial class meetings. Focus your attention on what happened and why as well as on what can or should be done the next time the situation arises. Such class meetings will set children on the road to taking on responsibility for reacting to situations they encounter outside of the class meeting in much the same way. Children will begin to internalize the questioning processes and start to ask before they act:

- **What did I do?**
- **Why did I do it?**
- **What could I have done instead?**
- **What will I do next time?**

> After I'd been teaching for a few years, I felt that I had become fairly proficient in communicating expectations, promoting social responsibility, and empowering students to be part of creating "our" classroom community. When conflicts erupted, I modeled the role of mediator and helped students resolve the issue, based on our classroom norms of respect and safety. At some point it occurred to me that I probably didn't need to play this mediator role as often as I did, and that the students could take responsibility for resolving their social conflicts. From then on, whenever I became aware of a brewing or full-fledged verbal conflict, I quickly sized it up with regard to the participants and the apparent level of intensity. If it seemed safe to use the strategy, I would approach the students and say, "It looks to me like you can probably work this out on your own. What do you think? You have 5 minutes to talk quietly over here (in a location I could safely monitor from a distance in case I'd misjudged the situation) and then rejoin us. If you decide you can't work it out, just let me know and we'll make a time for all of us to meet when it won't interrupt our learning. Sound okay?" Depending on the students' body language and responses, I'd assess how to proceed. This intervention took all of 30 seconds on my part, and I was amazed at how often it worked, even with students who had so-called "behavior disorders." Students reached resolution faster without my adult attention and interference, the rest of us could continue what we were doing, and the students with the conflict only lost 5 minutes of their instructional time instead of a much longer kind of "time out." When the time was up, I'd do a quick check in with each student. Unless the issue was connected to some serious infraction, there was no need for any further follow-up or consequences. The matter was simply over and done! Occasionally, I would even suggest that students consult with others who had successfully resolved a similar conflict.
>
> —Beth McDonald; New York University; New York, New York

Section 2

Whatever the situation, it is of utmost importance that you work to maintain the dignity of the students involved. Publicly humiliating a child is not an effective way of dealing with a problem as it will only lead to resentment of you and an increase in tension between that student, you, and the classroom community. Emotion is so closely linked to attention and learning that teachers cannot afford to violate a child in that manner as it will certainly diminish his or her learning potential both in relation to this specific behavioral situation and his or her academic learning in general (Caine and Caine 1997; Jensen 1995).

In the midst of a major behavioral incident, remember to recognize not only the child causing the problem but also the rest of the class. Remain calm and do not allow your response to elevate to a reactive level. If the child is being physically harmful to others, you must decide whether to move the other children or to remove the child causing the problem. Such a decision is best made on a case-by-case basis. Children who are of such a violent nature are already, or should be, known to the special services support team within that school, and that team will be able to best advise and support you as to how to handle such situations. It is critical that you remain exceptionally calm at all times. It would also be wise to work with the rest of the students at another time on how they should most appropriately act if the situation arises again. This is best done through a class meeting that may or may not involve the student in question. It would be wise to have that child involved, but depending on the specific parameters of that situation, it may not be appropriate or possible. Again, this is best addressed through the professional support staff on site.

For the most part, behavior problems within the classroom are rarely as intense as this, and, although they may disrupt teaching and learning, most behavior problems do not result in physical injury or threat to others.

As stated in the introduction, "Good management, like good teaching, is a matter of solving problems and helping people do their best. This too takes time and effort and thought and patience and talent" (Kohn 1993, 16). Good management does not come about as a result of a fancy sticker chart or reward system. It does not come about as a result of punishment or threat. Good management comes about as a result of time invested into establishing routines, procedures, and thoughtful ways of co-existing within the classroom.

Section 3: Managing Independent Work Time

Effective teachers know that they must provide students with activities that will allow them to work independently for up to an hour, so that teachers can pull small groups for instruction. Independent work includes students working alone, in partners, or in small groups on activities of their choice or activities assigned by teachers. When used optimally, independent work time requires little effort on the teacher's part outside of initially establishing routines and choices.

Typically, centers or stations are designated areas where students are assigned a specific task or can choose from several activities. In this section, the terms centers, stations, choices, and independent work are all used. Wheter a teacher utilizes a more teacher-directed center or station approach, or a less structured "choice" or independent work approach is dependent upon that teacher's comfort level with student-led decision making and the needs of the students. Regardless of which approach you choose, or which label you use, remember that they are places where students can work independently from teachers.

If you dedicate the first several weeks of the school year to establishing routines and a cohesive classroom community, toward the end of that four-week window, it will become clear when your students are ready to take on greater responsibility in working independently. It is important to note that each classroom is unique in and of itself and not all classes will arrive at this point simultaneously.

One of the best ways to ensure that independent work is a meaningful learning experience is to create a well-organized system. This section will help you create a management system that works for your particular situation as well as provides numerous ideas for creating and organizing independent work opportunities in your classroom that are meaningful and purposeful for the students, but that require little ongoing effort from the teacher.

Chapter 6

Management Systems

The organization of independent work time depends on the unique characteristics represented by each classroom. A poorly managed classroom that is characterized by a lack of routine will not provide an environment conducive to independent work or productive learning. Teachers must take time and care to coordinate the procedures that will result in a smoothly running operation if they expect their students to work independently from the teacher (Danielson 1996).

If you expect your students to be successful in working independently from you, you will need to establish a system that will allow them to work without your having to redirect their behavior constantly. Whether they happen to be more formally assigned centers and stations, or more open-ended, children-driven choices, independent work structures require a management system to ensure students understand where they should be and what they should be doing.

This chapter provides an overview of various management systems. They are organized into two sections: those that are more teacher directed and those that are more student directed. One system is not better than another—you will have to choose the system that will work best for you and your students. In the appendix you will find blackline masters that will help you construct the chart or coordinate the system you have chosen to use as a framework for organizing your students' independent work efforts.

> *I made the mistake of trying someone else's system without giving it enough thought. I had used the Stations chart (explained later in this chapter) for three years with slight modifications each year but with great success every year. All was well until I read an exceptional book by a fellow teacher who was using a very different system. I figured, she is so brilliant and successful, I better drop my system and use hers instead. So I did—and I struggled for months. Finally, I went to my principal to beg for help. For the life of me, I could not figure out what was wrong. She had no problem pointing out that the system I had discarded was one that had worked for me. "Good for you for exploring something new," she said. "But it is obviously not working. Why use it? You tried it, now go back to what works for you." —Lisa*

After reviewing the following models, decide which of them you are most comfortable with.

With all of these options, be flexible with how you group your students. Expect that your groups will change throughout the year, and do not organize students by ability. There may be times when you might organize students by ability for small group reading instruction; however, grouping students by ability often does not work well for independent work at assigned centers or stations. Instead, try to establish balanced groups in which students will support one another and you.

If you choose to use a rotating station management system, you might consider not changing stations on a rigid time schedule. It is nearly

Chapter 6: Management Systems

impossible to coordinate stations perfectly so that every child will start and finish at the same time. If you do choose to do this, be sure to have a backup plan for students who finish early or do not finish at all. Establishing yourself as a station may not be a good idea either, as that would require groups to rotate with their reading group families, giving them few opportunities to interact with the full range of students within your classroom.

Take the necessary time to introduce your system slowly—you can always speed up later if you want to. "Better safe than sorry" is a good motto here.

Two Systems, Two Successes

I made the mistake one year of trying to do "too much, too soon" in providing my students independent work time. I set up all the choices at once, explained them all, and let them go, expecting that things would run smoothly. As you can imagine, things did not go as I had planned and I had to act quickly. Rather than faulting my students for not performing as I had expected, I took the blame myself as I had not set my students up for success. Pulling the reins back in, I "closed" all of my independent station options and decided to open only one at a time, working with my students to ensure that they could work successfully there, and then going on to another one. I began by allowing only four students to work at a station at a time, while all the others continued to work with me in the whole group lesson. As a whole group, we would preview the station, identifying possible trouble areas and troubleshooting how we would handle any problems. After the four students completed their independent work, they would report back to the group, letting us know how things had gone, making suggestions for when the others would be there, and posing new dilemmas for us to work through as a group. Each group of students would have the same opportunity to work through each station in this manner, resulting in every child being able to work successfully in an independent fashion at that station. By presenting the stations to the whole group and having them work through them in small groups before offering them as independent choice options, I was able to ensure that every child would be successful. As time progressed, I introduced more station options, allowed more students to work independently at the same time, and lengthened the independent work time. —Lisa

During the first weeks of school, I introduced stations one at a time to the whole class. I would explicitly teach my students about the station—where to put this or how to use that, depending on what the station entailed. Then, we would all work in that station together for the first, and, possibly, second time, according to the needs of the group. Having each child working on the same station task at once allowed me to better monitor behaviors, and it gave my students an opportunity to practice the procedures they had just

(continued)

Section 3

learned. Once I felt that my students had mastered the station well enough to operate independently, we would move on to the next station, until every student was familiar with all of the stations. It was at this point that I would introduce the management system I chose to utilize, the Station Rotation Wheel. (This system is explained later on in this chapter.) In order to make sure that students remembered the operating procedures for each station, we would regularly go back and revisit the stations to refresh our memories. —Sarah

Teacher-Led Management Systems

The management systems in this section provide you with a greater amount of input regarding the choices your students make. Students work independently; however, you direct them to the tasks they should attend to.

Work Board

Work boards are tools that you can use to coordinate the movement of students through stations that you have selected. Within each station, there may be choices students can make; however, you are in charge of determining which stations students will visit on any given day.

To create a work board, first place children in groups, balancing out strong and struggling students, behavior problems and pacifists, etc., and record each group on index cards or sticky notes that can be placed on the work board. In the columns going down the chart, place a card with an icon directing children to the stations they are responsible for working in that day. Every day, simply move the group cards one space to the left or right and students have a whole new set of activities to work on.

There are several options within this management system. You may choose

Work Board

Group 1	Group 2	Group 3	Group 4
Sarah	Jon	Michael	Caroline
John	Karen	Bobby	Oscar
Elaine	Teddy	Mary	Cindy
Colleen	Nina	Beth	Jason
Dana	Scotty	Joe	Stella
Reading	Writing	Computer	Social Studies
Science	Choice	Math	Word Zone
Math	Social Studies	Reading	Writing
Computer	Word Zone	Science	Choice

Chapter 6: Management Systems

to have children rotate through the stations when prompted at predetermined intervals, or allow children to progress through at their own pace. Both of these decisions pose challenges that must you must consider. First, if you choose to move children from station to station at specified intervals, you must consider how to organize each station so that it ends at the same time or have a plan for what to do if students finish too early or too late. On the other hand, if you allow children to move through at their own pace, it would be wise to spend considerable time working with the students on how to pace themselves and what to do if they finish all their stations before independent work time is over.

A final consideration with this system is whether you want to designate yourself as a station for reading groups to rotate through. This option is easier for planning purposes, but remember that locking yourself into a station requires that students are always working within their ability groups, which makes it difficult for them to support one another as effectively as possible. You will also find that the timetable will ultimately revolve around your groups, and you will be unable to leave that group to assist other students in need.

Initially, you may want to have students work at only one station on any given day. When they have demonstrated successful work behavior, you can start to introduce additional stations, so that they ultimately work through three or four on any given day. You can also increase the amount of time students are working independently as you continue to release greater and greater responsibility to them as time goes on.

In the appendix, you will find a selection of icons that can be used to construct the work board of your choice. Have fun with these suggestions and come up with the one that will work best for you.

> Even though I work aggressively to make sure that my students are well-prepared to work independently, and I trust them implicitly, I also understand that they are eight- and nine-year-old children! As my children work independently and I pull small groups, I always situate myself and my group so that they sit with their backs to the rest of the room, and I am facing the remainder of the students, keeping an eye on them, just in case. —Sarah

Station Rotation Wheel

A simple way in which to organize stations and students is through the use of a rotation wheel. Some teachers choose to have two wheels, one smaller than the other, that are stacked on top of one another concentrically. The outer wheel has the different groups labeled; the inner wheel has the different station options. On a daily basis, the teacher simply rotates the wheel one position and each group is aligned with a new station.

> *Initially, I found that the Station Rotation Wheel worked for both my students and me— it was simple and easy and consistent. What did not work for me was the fact that my "wheel" kept falling apart! The system worked; the hardware didn't! I remedied the situation by tossing the back wheel out and labeling clothespins with my groups. I simply attached a clothespin to each of the sections of the wheel and rotated the clothespins on a daily basis. No more hardware problems!* —Sarah

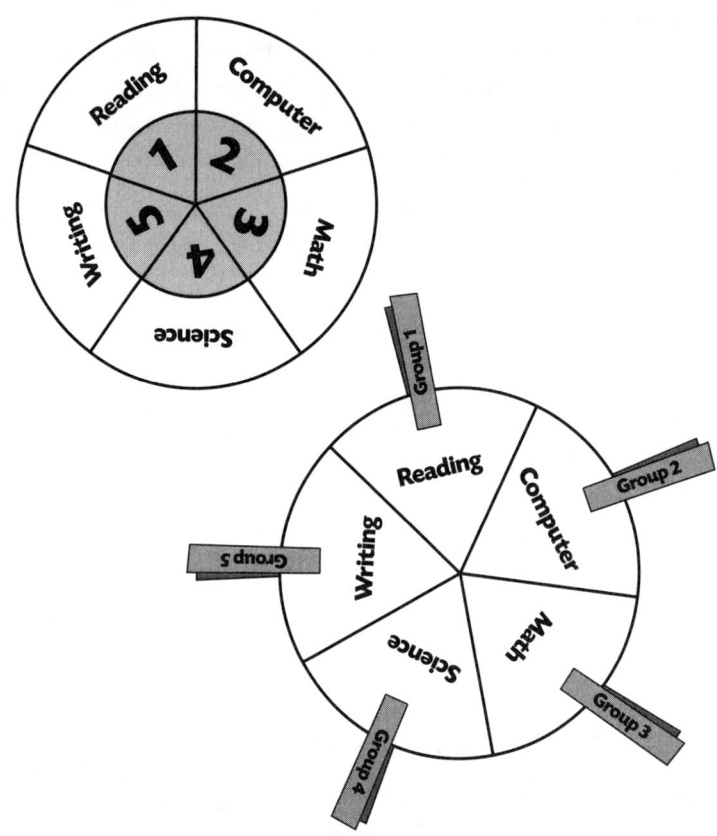

Stations Chart

This method provides a healthy balance between teacher direction and student choice. The Station Groups chart is a small one to be posted next to the larger "Stations" chart. It is a reference tool that identifies which students are in which group for that time period. (Work groups are usually good for a month or so, and then need to be changed.) You may want to laminate a copy and write names onto each shape with a washable pen so that it can be changed and reused every month or so.

In this model, children work in only one designated station every day and then are free to make their own choices once their work at that station is completed. (Rotating through all five stations every day would mean that you would have to create twenty-five stations a week!) The "Stations" chart identifies which group will be working at each station for that day. The next day, simply move the bottom number to the top and shift all the others down one space. For example, on the Monday chart in the illustration, the students in the Square group are working at Station #1, the students in the Rectangle group are working at Station #2, and so on. On Tuesday, the Rectangle group works at Station #1,

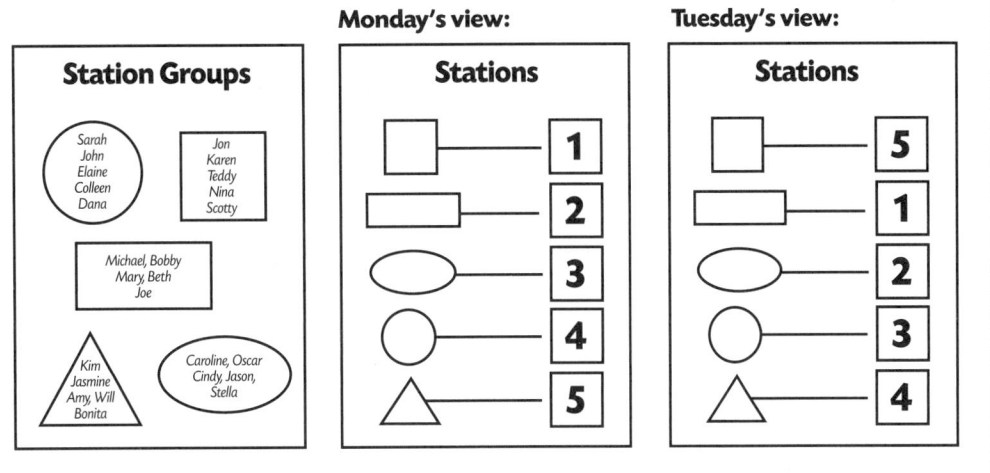

and so on. By the end of a five-day cycle, each group will have worked at each station. To make it easy for students to find materials, you may want to label tubs, boxes, or baskets with the corresponding station number. For example, place Station #1 materials in a tub marked Station #1.

This model is beneficial for teachers who are comfortable with students making their own choices but are still looking for more accountability or some measure of control. By rotating students through one station every day of the week, you can be assured that each student spends quality time with each activity.

Student-Directed Management Systems

After introducing a large number of independent work options, you may find that your group is sophisticated enough to make responsible choices during station time and that you can trust them to work purposefully for a designated amount of time. However, most teachers find that they need more structure than simply allowing students pure free choice. The following choices allow teachers to provide students with a considerable amount of freedom and responsibility, yet still allow some degree of teacher direction and monitoring of the choices that are made.

Today's Choices

This is simply a list or a space on a bulletin board indicating independent work choices for that day. For example, a teacher may decide to have students work independently choosing from six or eight stations and can simply list those choices. Obviously, there would be fewer choices at the beginning of the year, and the list of options would expand as more choices were made available to the students.

Limitations to this system relate to children's level of maturity and responsible behavior. Also remember that for students to have choices, you need to have already introduced a large number of station activities and to make sure that children are very comfortable with them.

Open/Closed

Another manner of indicating which choices are available is to simply attach a two-sided card to each set of station materials or station area—one side labeled "Open," the other "Closed." As children go to use the stations, they must first check whether that choice is available to them that day.

A variation of this system would be to post a large poster listing all of the choices or stations. After each one, place a two-sided card with Open on one side and Closed on the other. Use the cards next to the name of each station to indicate its status for that day.

Today's Choices

	Classroom Library	Open
	Reading	Open
	Writing	Open
	Art	Closed
	Listening	Open
	Math	Open
	Science	Open
	Word Zone	Closed

Contracts

Contracts are similar to the above systems as children are free to make their own choices, but require that they record their own work efforts. Take care not to use this system in a manner that results in too much work for yourself. The purpose of having a contract is to help the children self-direct their behavior. Some teachers find that it is beneficial to use these items with all of their students to help them self-monitor their choices, but many teachers find that they are unnecessary for most of their students and use them only with the few students struggling to make good choices.

Some teachers use contracts as a self-monitoring tool as well as a powerful assessment tool that can be used in conferences with children and parents in discussing work habits. Different versions of contracts are included in the appendix for you to choose from, each providing the student with slightly different levels of support.

Class Lists

Create an alphabetical class list of the first and/or last names of your students (depending on their age) in a large size font. Copy dozens of these on brightly colored paper and laminate them for use in all stations. Children can indicate that they have used that station by crossing off their name or recording the date using a water-based overhead projector pen. These lists become a good monitoring tool as you check to see which children are using which stations, redirecting student choices as needed. They are also helpful for students who all want to use the same station. By consulting the list, they can see who has or has not had a turn at that station, or whose turn was most recent, and decide from there which student should have priority.

Efficiency and Effectiveness Task

Choosing Your Own System

Go back through the chapter and think about which of these systems is most appealing to you, based on your experience and comfort with independent work. After determining which system is the one you think you will implement this year, share your thoughts with a friend, asking for his or her thoughts and advice. Keep in mind that you are making this initial decision without knowing your students. During the first few weeks of school, as you get to know them better, come back to this decision and re-evaluate it. Is that system really the best choice now that you know your students better? If the knowledge you have gained about the chemistry in your classroom this years suggests that you change your initial decision, now is the time to do so!

Chapter 7

Organizing Stations with Engaging Activities

A well-managed classroom is one in which both teachers and students are able to work effectively. If a teacher is to work effectively with small groups, the rest of the students will have to be engaged with stations or other appropriate independent work activities. Ensuring that tasks are manageable and meaningful will greatly enhance the likelihood of this taking place. Using the management system of your choice from the previous chapter, all of the activities in this chapter will find a comfortable home in the midst of a meaningful and productive independent work period in your classroom.

Independent work time will look differently at each grade level and within each classroom. It is important to provide students with a range of station choices and options within each station that match the unique range of learners within that classroom. This chapter provides numerous station activities that you can use for small group or individual work efforts. Base the activities you choose on the needs of your learners.

It is important to consider seriously the choices you offer students for station activities. They should not be viewed as a way to keep children busy or as an opportunity for students to learn new or unfamiliar content. For independent work time to be successful, teachers must provide choices that

- **are open-ended,**
- **provide for a range of ability levels,**
- **are of high interest,**
- **are meaningful and purposeful to the child,**
- **require very little, if any, photocopying,**
- **do not require extensive teacher preparation,**
- **do not necessitate comprehensive teacher grading and evaluation, and**
- **provide students an opportunity to practice and reinforce both known and developing literacy skills and strategies.**

The best stations are those that are open-ended and that children can and will revisit over and over again. It would be easy to simply run off a packet of work sheets filled with meaningless activities; however, such activities do not help children learn to read or write (Smith 1986). "It will not be productive (or even efficient) for children to be doing busy work like coloring or fill-in-the-blank worksheets. Research does not support such activities, and too much learning time is lost when the management plan relies on them" (Fountas and Pinnell 1996, 53). Working at stations that provide authentic reading and writing practice on students' independent level is far more beneficial in assisting children to learn to read and write (Holdaway 1979).

It is important to recognize that stations are not necessarily a place children go to work; they refer more accurately to what children are doing. For example, a writing station may not actually be a location in the room but instead a tub full of materials related to writing. Many classroom teachers find that their space is limited physically. Do not let that undermine your efforts to provide your students with opportunities to work independently.

The station ideas on the following pages are designed to be authentic literacy tasks. Each one is designed so you have a host of activities with a range of levels to introduce to students over time. They also require no time standing in line at the copy machine and are open-ended activities that can and will be joyfully repeated time and time again. The students are left to practice enthusiastically, using their developing set of literacy skills and strategies, and the teacher is left to teach.

Each of the stations is organized into two main sections:

- **Materials to Include**
- **Activities to Do**

The Materials to Include list is merely a list of suggested items to include. Do not feel as if your station will be inadequate if you do not have every one of the listed items. As a matter of fact, as you start to stock these stations, you may find that you have far more materials than those suggested. In the Activities to Do section, there are suggested activities that many teachers have used successfully. Be sure to introduce the activities slowly and only offer those that are well within the independent range of your students.

Classroom Library

According to Richard Allington (2001), by the end of third grade, good readers are reading ten times as many words a day as poor readers. It is imperative that teachers organize a time for children to read on a daily basis (unless teachers are certain that students are reading regularly and voraciously outside of school). It is not acceptable to have free reading available as a choice only for students who complete their work early. Those in greatest need of additional exposure to books will receive even less and the gap between their peers will widen even further.

Following are a variety of ideas that you can incorporate into your library corner, providing opportunities that extend beyond simply reading a book. Refer to section 1 for more information on how to organize and set up your classroom library.

Materials to Include

The following are some materials you may want to include in your classroom library. Feel free to add or delete items as you feel is appropriate for your students.

• **Old favorites** (books you have read aloud that are class favorites)
• **Texts at grade level**
• **Texts below grade level**
• **Texts above grade level**
• **Small versions of Big Books**
• **Fiction texts**
  – Fantasy
  – Science Fiction
	• **Nonfiction texts**
	  – Encyclopedia
	  – Dictionary
	  – Reference
	  – Expository
	  Informative:
	  Description, History, Interview
	  Explanatory:
	  Procedural, how to; Question and answer; Compare and contrast; Cause and effect; Problem and solution
		– Narrative
		  Narrative account, Biography, Personal profile, Journal
		– Persuasive
		  Debate
		• **Students' published books**
		• **Magazines**
		• **Pamphlets and flyers** (found in hotels and tourist information centers)
			• **Menus**
			• **Phone books**
			• **Catalogs**
			• **Big Books** (and matching small books, as available)
			• **Newspapers**
			• **Sticky notes, paper, and writing utensils**
			• **Book repair supplies** (tape, etc.)

Activities to Do

The following are some suggested activities for the classroom library. Choose the activities that are most appropriate for your students.

Individual and/or Buddy Reading

Allow students to read quietly to themselves, or have students take turns reading from the same book.

Book Clubs or Literature Circles

Teach proficient readers to form book clubs or literature circles within your small reading group instruction. Proficient readers are capable of having high-level conversations about the books they are reading after experiencing such conversations multiple times within the more formal teacher-led reading group.

Book Reviews

Provide students the opportunity to write recommendations for books they really enjoy. Several well-known bookstores do something similar: The employees choose their most recent favorite book and tell why they like it or who might enjoy it. They then display the reviews for customers to browse through. In a classroom, you might organize a low bulletin board to be covered with resealable bags, one for each child. Students can choose to write a recommendation on their card and slip both the card and the book into the pocket for others to browse through.

Book Hospital

Have a book hospital (Webb 1999) available for students to repair well-used and loved books. Teach students how to use packing tape to repair the binding of much-loved books and to use tape to mend torn pages. Books should stay in the book hospital until the main doctor (the teacher) reviews the patient (the book) and releases it back to the library. Keeping books in the hospital overnight allows you to monitor the system to make sure it is not being misused.

Parts of a Book or Magazine

Use children's magazines and other high interest materials to provide opportunities for students to explore and learn about indexes, tables of contents, skimming and scanning text, and other features of nonfiction text. You may also allow children to organize for your next unit by putting together a bibliography of resources from the school library.

Take a Trip

Collect all the travel brochures you can find in hotels, highway service areas, airports, etc. These texts provide students with an opportunity to explore the world around them in a very realistic fashion. Students can also work together to create realistic uses of these materials. For example, two students might work together to figure out how much it would cost to take their family to a theme park for the day.

Categories Game

This activity is based on the game Scattegories®. Start a file box of index cards, with one section per unit/theme. Have students generate categories such as "Things the Pilgrims Ate" or "The United States." Have students work individually, in pairs, or in teams to generate words that fall in the chosen category. These can then be used as independent, small group, or whole class content review lessons.

The Question Game

This activity is based on the games Jeopardy® and Trivial Pursuit®. Start a file box of index cards, with one section per unit/theme. Have students generate questions and answers on opposite sides of the card. To play, have one child read the answer and the other one create an appropriate question. For example, the answer might be "A shape with three sides of identical length." The question would be "What is an equilateral triangle?" A variation of this game is to have children read the question and then provide the answer, using the same cards.

Poetry Station

There are four text types that teachers need to incorporate into reading instruction on a regular basis: fiction, nonfiction, familiar rereads, and poetry. It is unfortunate that this final text type is often destined to appear only during a poetry unit. Do not overlook or underestimate the value of poetry. Poetry is a powerful form of writing that allows the author to communicate a great deal of feeling and meaning, using very few words relative to the message delivered by the poem.

The apparent simplicity of poetry is often appealing to students as it does not appear threatening to them and is so varied that it can be enjoyed by everyone. A poetry station is a relatively easy one to establish and maintain but quite powerful in its simplicity, just like the poems it stands to represent.

Within a poetry station, children need the opportunity to explore poetry freely by investigating and manipulating existing poems and creating their own original works. A well-designed poetry station will encompass both the reading and writing of poetry. The informal nature of the poetry station will also support students in their exploration of this genre as "poetry is a craft in which the first impressions of the poet are the most important" (Groeber 2001, 8).

Materials to Include

The following are some materials you may want to include in your poetry station. Feel free to add or delete items as you feel is appropriate for your students.

- **Published poetry collections and anthologies**
- **Class-selected poetry collections and anthologies** (students' favorite poems kept in binders)
- **Examples and templates for specific poetry forms** that have been explored within the classroom
- **Poetry, rhyme charts, and posters**
- **Copies of favorite poems** that the teacher has written on chart paper
- **Printed version of class songs**
- **Wiki Stix highlighting tape, or pieces of see-through, removable book covers** for identifying features of text on charts
- **Pointers** for tracking text
- **Paper and writing utensils** for students to write their own poetry

Activities to Do

The following are some suggested activities for the poetry station. Choose the activities that are most appropriate for your students.

Individual and/or Buddy Reading

Have students read poems alone or with a partner.

Look and Find

Have children work in partners to identify and label features of text. For example, one child says, "Find all the similes," and the other child proceeds to mark each example with highlighting tape. The possibilities are endless here as children take on the teacher's role with their peers.

Poem Puzzles

Choose some favorite class poems. Create two copies of the poem. Glue one copy to the front of a large mailing envelope, and cut up the second copy line by line. Place the cut-up poem pieces inside the envelope. Students can use the lines of the poem as puzzle pieces that they have to put together. They can use the original poem to check accuracy.

Students can also try to organize the lines without looking at the complete poem. Provide time to discuss the decisions they made as they work to construct a meaningful poem, then compare their poem to the original.

Writing or Rewriting Poetry

Ask students to write poems such as haikus, acrostics, and so on. You might also have students rewrite poems with different endings or rewrite classic nursery rhymes as stories, including more detail, dialogue, etc.

Poetry Reading

Have students recite familiar poems, dramatizing them with or without the use of props. You might also encourage students to select favorite poems to memorize and present at a class poetry reading.

Writing Station

The best way to support and develop students as writers is to provide opportunities to write often, widely, and freely. Children who are limited to only writing for others, at their direction, and on their topics are not truly writers (Graves 1994). One responsibility of a teacher of writing is to model for children a wide range of topics and text types. Within the writing station, be sure to include every possible writing surface and implement you can possibly get your hands on, and allow for student choice in their topics. It is also important to remember that this independent work time is an opportunity for students to practice their developing skills related to literacy. You can certainly use the items students write for assessment purposes to help direct future instruction or as a focus for conferencing, but do not feel the need to take home all student work from this station to be graded.

Materials to Include

The following are some materials you may want to include in your writing station. Feel free to add or delete items as you feel is appropriate for your students.

- All shapes, sizes, and colors of paper
- Writing utensils
- Office supplies
- Miniature white boards or chalkboards
- Stationery
- Dictionaries
- Thesauruses
- Writing reference guides
- Class lists
- School directory
- Index cards
- Sticky notes
- Envelopes
- Clipboards

Activities to Do

The following are some suggested activities for the writing station. Choose the activities that are most appropriate for your students.

Writing Lists

Writing lists allows children to record their ideas without concern for complete sentences or text coherence. It can also double as an informal comprehension and spelling assessment. The lists can be serious or fun—the point is to have students generate several ideas quickly and capture them on paper. The following are some examples of possible lists:

- Grocery lists (try using newspaper ads)
- Lists of items for a birthday, Mother's Day, or Christmas
- Things to pack
- Animals
- Things that have to do with Africa
- Excuses for not doing homework
- Reasons for going to the nurse

Picture Writing

Use photographs or pictures cut from magazines and ask children to generate a story quickly from the images. This allows students to dedicate their energies to recording a story without having to spend time thinking up a topic. You may think that these picture writing opportunities are somewhat similar to blackline masters many teachers use; however, the entire class is not assigned a single picture to write about. Instead, every child chooses her or his own. This is an excellent example of a station that is differentiated for varied levels of students. There will be intermediate students for whom each of these activities is appropriate. Make sure to build an extensive picture file so students can easily find pictures that suit them. See the Using Pictures to Prompt Writing (see appendix for full blackline master) for writing ideas.

Tally Chart

Put up a laminated chart or dry erase board that can be reused, and divide it in half. On one side, write one statement, and write the opposite statement on the other side. For example, write "I agree with the decision Rosa Parks made on the bus in Montgomery, Alabama" and "I disagree with the decision Rosa Parks made on the bus in Montgomery, Alabama." Have students record their responses by adding their name or by making a tally mark on the side they agree with. Once all students have recorded their beliefs, discuss the findings as a whole class.

Once students are comfortable with this activity, make class lists or paper for their own surveys available. After collecting and analyzing their data, students can follow up on their findings with additional research and, ultimately, present their findings to the class, orally, visually, or in writing.

Sticky Note Posters

Write a thought-provoking statement or question (age appropriate, of course) on poster board or chart paper. Then give students sticky notes and ask them to write a response and place it on the poster or chart paper. Give students a few days to respond, then review the responses with the whole group. Pretty soon, you may find that children are writing their own questions.

Some examples of questions you might use are shown at the right.

> **Do you think students should be allowed to have common fast food items as a choice in the cafeteria? Why or why not?**

> **What do you suppose would have happened if Little Ann hadn't died in *Where the Red Fern Grows*?**

Message Board

Provide paper for students to write messages to one another. After writing a message to a peer, the child folds it in half, writes the other student's name on the front, and attaches it to a bulletin board. At the end of the day, allow one student to deliver any messages that have not been picked up. Written conversations such as these are powerful opportunities for children to experience functional writing (Harste, Short, and Burke 1988).

Post Office

Similar to the Message Board activity, students have the opportunity to write to other students—either within their class or in other classes. In-class mail can be placed in student mailboxes; out-of-class mail can be organized by homeroom and delivered at the end of the day.

Letter Writing

You might consider including postage stamps on children's beginning of the year school supply lists. Children can choose to write letters to individuals or parties and send them via the U.S. Mail.

Class Surveys

Allow children to create their own surveys and then poll their classmates. Using one of the class lists, children can collect and record data. Be sure to have students summarize all the information they learned. For example, a student might survey her peers by asking, "Do you have a pet?" Depending on the child's purpose, she may simply record "Yes" or "No," or go on to request more detailed information as to the types and numbers of pets each child has. Children can summarize this information in a statement to the class, or they could even record it in the form of a student-generated graph.

Headline Writing

Provide pictures from newspapers, magazines, old history texts, or your photo album, and ask students to write captions or headlines that spark interest. You may choose to have a "Picture of the Week" that every child provides headlines for, or you may just have a collection of them in a book that children can add to throughout the year.

Powerful Leads

This activity is similar to the Headline Writing activity. In this activity, ask children to suggest powerful leads for a story that might be written in connection with the picture.

Catalogs

Take out all the descriptive words and phrases from the catalog descriptions, leaving the item descriptors very banal, and have children rewrite them. Or, let kids use pictures and create their own catalogs, writing their own creative descriptions for each item.

If you have catalogs that support specific populations (e.g., children, runners, or campers), let children use them as models to create unique catalogs of their choice. For example, students might want to create a catalog for Antarctic explorers, the first colonists on Mars, or orangutans.

Letters to...

Collect advice letters from the newspaper and have children write responses to the "Dear Abby" type letters. Or, allow children to create their own requests for advice and let other children respond to the letters.

Story Problems

Mathematical story problems are a lot more fun when you can relate to them. Allow children to create their own and share them with other students to solve.

Where Am I?

Allow students to direct each other from one location to another on a map by providing a written set of instructions. The first child needs to designate a starting point, and then provide step-by-step written directions for which roads to travel. The second child follows the directions and compares his or her final destination to the location the direction giver intended. These can be left in the station for other students to reuse, only be sure to have students record the ultimate destination on a key or on the back of the set of directions.

Using the maps as models, you might also have students create their own map of a fictional location from their reading.

Penmanship Station

Although handwriting and penmanship are best taught through authentic writing in which neatness is important to both the writer and the reader for effective communication, it is valuable to provide opportunities for students to practice these skills. Students need to learn to print and write script legibly. Why not make it purposeful and fun? It is important to catch and correct any improper letter formation and grips as early as possible if it is to be corrected. An excellent support resource for this purpose is the school or district occupational therapist.

Materials to Include

The following are some materials you may want to include in your handwriting/penmanship station. Feel free to add or delete items as you feel is appropriate for your students.

- **All shapes, sizes, and colors of paper** available, both with and without lines at all grade levels
- **Writing utensils** such as pens, pencils, crayons, chalk, markers
- **Miniature white boards or chalkboards**
- **Clipboards**
- **Easels**
- **Paintbrushes**
- **Handwriting models** (cursive or manuscript depending on the grade level)

Activities to Do

The following are some suggested activities for the handwriting/penmanship station. Choose the activities that are most appropriate for your students.

Free Writing

Have a variety of surfaces available for writing practice. You may need to remind children that these materials are available for them to practice their handwriting, not their drawing. White boards are especially nice because children can erase their mistakes without leaving a trace.

Signs/Advertisements

Charge your students with creating signs and posters that provide necessary information around the school.

Laminated Pages and "Lipstick Pens"

There is something magical about using water-based overhead pens—the tops of the pens are slanted like a lipstick, thus the name "lipstick pens." It seems that the usual boring and meaningless handwriting practice sheets that are copied and given to the whole class hold an entirely different value when just a few of each are laminated and used for practice with lipstick pens. You might also try copying them on colorful paper and cutting the pages into small strips to make the task more manageable and appealing.

Forms

Collect job applications and other forms (bank slips, sweepstakes forms, etc.) and encourage students to fill them out as neatly as possible.

Interviews

Create your own classroom information/interview sheets and have children interview one another, recording responses as neatly as possible so that they will be able to post their information for others to read.

Art Station

Children creating art pieces to decorate refrigerators is a brilliant way to develop small motor skills, learn about unique features and characteristics of different objects, and experience an enjoyable form of expression. Exploring the arts is critical in the development of any child. It is a valuable opportunity to introduce famous artists and their works. As each one is explored, students' repertoires of artistic expressions are expanded and that knowledge can be used as they create their own artwork.

Take caution not to spend too much time here if the artwork takes the form of coloring, cutting out, and pasting together an art project that started out as a blackline master and results in a class set of nearly identical products. True artistic responses are open-ended and do not require a copy machine.

> A friend and colleague of mine, John Slagle (2001) once commented to me, "How can cutting out a bunny and pasting a cotton ball on its behind help kids learn how to read?" I laughed. And I agreed. —Lisa

Slagle makes a valid point. If teaching children to read is the primary intention, it is important to make careful decisions regarding how to use instructional time. Try to avoid whole group art projects. Other than as an introduction to a task, using whole group time for an in-class art project is not the best use of instructional time. That time would be much better spent on an academic task of sorts, moving the art project into a station that all children have a chance to work through. An added bonus here is that clean up is much more manageable. Instead of having twenty-five children struggle to use glue, paint, or tissue paper at once, you only have a handful of children doing so and can easily call on other students for assistance in coordinating and cleaning up the project.

Materials to Include

The following are some materials you may want to include in your art station. Feel free to add or delete items as you feel is appropriate for your students. (Please note that it might not be a good idea to have all of these materials available all the time.) You can ask local businesses or parents to help with donations.

- **Paper**
  - Letter- or legal-size paper
  - Large white paper
  - Paper grocery bags
  - Tissue paper
- **Supplies**
  - Glue
  - Paint (tempera and water color)
  - Paint brushes
  - Scissors
- Markers
- Crayons
- Pencils
- Chalk
- Liquid chalk
- **Books**
  - Current art books
  - Art history books
  - Art method texts
  - Picture books of artists' styles

Activities to Do

The following are some suggested activities for the art station. Choose the activities that are most appropriate for your students. Be creative when setting up these activities. Use sponge paint, wash watercolor over crayon or chalk, put glitter in a mixture of glue and water to make "glittery glue paint," or use watered-down glue to make tissue paper collages.

Artwork for Books

Have children re-illustrate a favorite picture book. Type up the words (or let the children do so) and let children make a class-illustrated version of a favorite text. Or, have students create an innovation on a favorite text, and then illustrate and publish it as a class book or a mural.

Hink Pinks

Another option is to have students create a book of idioms, nonfiction text features, or Hink Pinks (Cunningham 1995), which are rhyming word pairs, such as "fat cat" or "pink drink." (Hinky-Pinkys and Hinkety Pinketys are the same, but have two or three syllables respectively.) Each child (or pair) is responsible for illustrating his or her own page to be added to a class book. If you would like for every child to have his or her own copy, consider having children draw the pictures with a thick black pen. Photocopy the class set and make books for students to keep.

Illustrate Environmental Print

Have children make illustrations for shared- and modeled-writing texts to be posted in the room. Do your kids love a poem in a small book? Enlarge the text by writing it on chart paper and put them in charge of the accompanying illustration. This may be a group or individual effort.

Journals

Let children draw pictures of things they might want to write about in their journals. When it is time to write, they can get right to work.

Word Zone

This section includes a variety of activities that can also be used for a vocabulary station. As children begin to work with and explore letters and words and how they are structured, they will be better prepared to use their graphophonic knowledge as they read and write. All of the activities have been designed to provide authentic and engaging opportunities to explore different phonetic, orthographic, and etymological elements and concepts.

Materials to Include

Listed at the right are some materials you may want to include in the word zone. Feel free to add or delete items as you feel is appropriate for your students.

- Magnetic letters
- Class lists
- Cards with individual students' names
- Dictionary
- Thesaurus
- Small letter lines
- Games and activities related to letters and words

Activities to Do

The following are some suggested activities for the word zone. Choose the activities that are most appropriate for your students, remembering the needs of struggling readers.

Magnetic Letters

Have students sort letters by putting together the alphabet or by finding all the tall letters, short letters, vowels, letters with humps. You can also ask them to make lists of words (friends, colors, etc.), create word families (the "at" family includes "at," "cat," "sat," "mat," "hat"), or put together word trains (do*g-gras*s-*sun-n*ose...).

For a fun phonemic awareness activity, they can substitute the correct letter for the letter of their choice, creating an entirely new "word." For example, "Mike" would be recorded as "-ike" and students could substitute different letters, creating both real and nonsense words such as "hike," "like," "rike," and "zike." (Note: You can easily organize and store magnetic letters in tackle boxes or shoe boxes.)

Matching Games

Matching games include having students match words to pictures, letters to pictures, capital letters to lowercase letters, manuscript to cursive writing, and so on. You can also use old flash cards, magazine pictures, or bulletin board borders cut apart to play well-known card games such as Old Maid, Go Fish, or Memory.

Newspaper Searches

Encourage children to use a newspaper to hunt for words in different categories (e.g., countries, people's names, adjectives, compound words, different words for "said," long *e* words, or two-syllable words). When children find a word that fits into the category either you or your students identified, they can either copy that word onto a piece of paper housing the collection or cut out the words and glue them onto a paper.

You can also have children search the newspaper for one-, two-, three-, or four-syllable words and sort them into categories by length. Children can either write the words or cut them out, but be sure to monitor the activity to make sure that it maintains its focus on words and does not turn into a cut and paste activity.

Fancy Words/Names

Let children choose a word they love or their name, write it poster size in bubble letters (you may need to this for younger students), and decorate it. Celebrate each word with the entire class, savoring its unique features.

The Name Game

Let children use their name or someone else's and find as many words as possible that can be made using the letters in that name. For example, one-letter words that can be made from "Lisa Elizabeth Renee Dellamora" include "I" and "a." Two-letter words include "be," "me," "is," etc. Some students find this task more manageable when they have letter cards or magnetic letters to manipulate.

Sniglets

Sniglets is a term coined by the popular television show "Saturday Night Live" for words they invented to match common objects or actions that did not already have a term or label. Children can have fun creating words and definitions for things that do not yet have labels (e.g., the film that covers the top of pudding might be called "shlick"). Encourage students to organize these definitions into a class dictionary of invented words.

Note: This is probably not a good activity for students who are English Language Learners.

Hink Pinks

Hink Pinks are rhyming word pairs, such as "fat cat" or "pink drink" (Cunningham 1995). Ask students to create riddles that other children can try to figure out. For example, the answer to "What is a chubby kitty?" could be a "fat cat" or a "flabby tabby." (Hinky-Pinkys and Hinkety Pinketys are the same, but have two and three syllables, respectively.)

Letter Cards/Tiles

Use one-inch ceramic floor tiles and write letters on them using permanent pens or dry erase pens. Have children use the tiles to make their full name (or someone else's) and then try to see how many words they can make and record using those letters.

Alphabetical Lists

Have children create an alphabetical list of words or phrases related to a given topic (e.g., challenges the Pilgrims faced, things in the room, foods, animals, and famous people). The challenge is for students to come up with something for each letter of the alphabet. To make it more challenging, have some students find two items for each letter, or ask them to make a list using only words with a given number of syllables.

A to Z Stories

Challenge students to write short stories that are alphabetical in nature. The first word must start with the letter A, the second word with the letter B, and so on. For example, "A big cat doesn't eat furry green hamburgers in . . ."

Alliterative Sentences

Tongue twisters are always fun to say and create. They also provide students with the opportunity to explore the phonetic element that remains constant through all or most of the sentence. Challenge children to generate all the words they can think of that begin with the same initial sound, and then construct a tongue twister using those words. For example, "Lainey loves to lick luscious lollipops!" or "Kirsten and Colleen can kiss quite a lot of kangaroos." Notice in the second example that although the initial letters are different, the sounds are the same.

Alphabet Books

Allow children to read alphabet books individually or with a partner. Make sure you have plenty available, such as *Q Is for Duck* (Etling 1980), *Tomorrow's Alphabet* (Shannon 1996), *The Z Was Zapped* (Van Allsburg 1987), Rigby's PM alphabet/ blend books, *Dr. Seuss' ABC* (Seuss 1963).

You also might want to invite students to write their own alphabet books. Children can create their own simple ones using pictures cut from old phonics books. Students can also work to create alphabet books linked to their content area studies (e.g., an alphabet book on the first Thanksgiving).

Content Area Word Activities

Generate a list of topic words and write each one on a separate index card. Then have children sort them into categories. Provide categories for a closed sort, or let children create their own categories for an open sort activity. An example would be the words "lion," "tuna," "monkey," "parrot," "frog," "alligator," and a list of other animals that students would be expected to sort either by habitat, dangerous/not dangerous to humans, or by the type of animal.

You also might ask students to build word ladders by listing topic-related words, starting with one-syllable words, then two-syllable words, then three, and so on.

Listening Station

Listening to stories read on tape provides children with several benefits. First, they are exposed to the fluent and expressive reading that they need to have modeled for them to take on the responsibility for such reading themselves. Secondly, children are able to listen to the reader as they follow along in the text, giving them an opportunity to match the spoken word to the written word as the narrator makes his or her way through the text as the child reads along. Many of the audiotapes available include music, songs, and activities related to the text that will further engage students.

Don Holdaway (1979) makes an interesting point about the audiotapes used in listening stations: "We use mainly male voices because many of the slower children are boys and they must not get the idea that reading is a feminine occupation. In our chauvinistic society, if they once begin to think of reading as sissy, they're in real trouble" (73). Even though society has come a long way since 1979, his point is still a valid one and gives teachers something to think about. Listed below are additional ideas to consider when organizing a listening station.

Materials to Include

Listed at the right are some materials you may want to include in your listening station. Feel free to add or delete items as you feel is appropriate for your students.

- **Books and poems** with matching audiotapes
- **Audiotapes** of the teacher doing lessons with books in the classroom
- **Cassette player**
- **Headphones**
- **Blank cassette tapes**
- **Resealable bags** to keep books with the accompanying tapes

Activities to Do

The following are some suggested activities for the listening station. Choose the activities that are most appropriate for your students.

Early and Emergent Readers

Students can listen to recordings of texts alone, with a partner, or in a small group. Some ideas for text recordings include the following:

- **Have parents, grandparents, the local fire chief, and other important individuals record themselves reading a text of their choice.**
- **Have various staff members record their favorite book.**
- **Tape yourself as you do a lesson.** Students will hear modeled reading, as well as have another opportunity to respond to the questions you ask.
- **Tape record your students singing or reading and provide the lyrics or text for them to follow.**
- **Let students earn the privilege of recording a favorite book on tape.** This is especially good for intermediate students who need to work on practicing fluency—they can practice a book, record it with sound effects, and then donate it to a primary classroom. This also provides the teacher with a valuable assessment tool documenting that student's reading.

Note: When recording, record the text over and over again on the tape so students do not have to rewind it constantly.

Transitional and Fluent Readers

Teach children how to create and record new songs linked to content area information by changing the words to familiar tunes (e.g., to the tune of "Row, Row, Row Your Boat," sing the Christopher Columbus song "Sail, sail, sail your ship. Sail it night and day. Look for land, look for land, all along the way"). You can also encourage children to create their own tunes, raps, etc., with lyrics matching content area studies. This is a great study tool for all students.

> **Efficiency and Effectiveness Task**
>
> **Gradually Adding Activities**
>
> Choose one station from the previous suggestions. Choose two activities from the station to introduce to your students. The following week, introduce two more. Once you have five to six activities, choose another station and begin introducing activities. Once you have all your stations in place, slowly add additional activities to each station.

Appendix

CONTENTS

How Does the Classroom Feel? 139	I'm Learning To . . . / I Can 149
How Does the Classroom Look? 140	Emergent Reading Checklist 150
How Does the Classroom Sound? 142	Early Reading Checklist 151
Peer Questions 143	Fluent Reading Checklist 152
What Is on Your Walls? 144	Teaching Routines Checklist 153
AM Schedule 145	Icons 154
PM Schedule 146	Group Icons 156
Small Reading Group Levels 147	Contract 157
Small Reading Group Notes 148	Using Pictures to Prompt Writing 158

Appendix

How Does the Classroom Feel?

Teacher: _____

Grade Level: _____ School Year: _____ Number of Students: _____

✔ Do I feel comfortable as I enter?

✔ Do I get a peaceful sense of order, or am I overwhelmed by a sense of chaos?

✔ Is this a place where I would enjoy spending six (give or take) hours a day? Would I want to learn here? Could I learn here?

✔ What appears to be important in this room?

✔ Is there an appropriate space for every student in the classroom?

Appendix

How Does the Classroom Look?

Teacher: _____

Grade Level: _____ School Year: _____ Number of Students: _____

✔ Is there a teacher's desk? If so, where is it? How and when is it used?

✔ How are the student desks or tables organized?

✔ What other large furniture items are in the classroom, and how are they arranged for optimal learning and movement?

✔ Are there logical pathways for movement?

✔ Is there a floor space large enough for intimate whole group instruction?

✔ Is there some place for children to work quietly?

✔ Are materials well organized and accessible?

How Does the Classroom Look? (continued)

- ✔ Is there an overabundance of workbooks and worksheets?

- ✔ Is there a lot of unnecessary clutter?

- ✔ Are there reference tools and resources readily available? How are they being used?

- ✔ What else is on the walls?

- ✔ Is there a classroom library? How is it organized?

- ✔ Are there clearly visible surfaces available for whole group writing instruction?

- ✔ Do students have a sense of how the environment has been organized?

Appendix

How Does the Classroom Sound?

Teacher: _____

Grade Level: _____ School Year: _____ Number of Students: _____

✔ Whose voices do I hear? What are they saying?

✔ Are the students and teacher aware of their own voices?

✔ How effectively can the teacher get students' attention?

Appendix

Peer Questions

Teacher: _____ Date _____

Have your peer answer or ask yourself the following questions:

- Where does the teacher position him- or herself for instruction?

- Is there a balance of voices in the room, or are only certain students and the teacher being heard?

- Is there an imposing feeling of control?

- Does the teacher go to the children or do the children have to go to the teacher?

- If the children go to the teacher, is there a long line of children constantly seeking help or approval?

- Is covering the content, regardless of student needs, an overshadowing characteristic?

- Physically, how are things organized?

- How does the teacher convey that books and reading are important? Are books easily accessible to students?

- How does the teacher honor children's work? Is the work visible?

- Do learners appear to be self-motivated and independent?

Appendix

What Is on Your Walls?

Fill out the following chart. As you go through your day, circle the items your students use or attend to regularly. Star the items you model the use of. After about a week, review your list and decide which materials on your walls are valuable instructional materials and which need to go.

Items I Purchased	**Things I Made**

Things I Made With My Students	**Things My Students Made**

AM Schedule

	Monday	Tuesday	Wednesday	Thursday	Friday
DATE					
8:00					
8:15					
8:30					
8:45					
9:00					
9:15					
9:30					
9:45					
10:00					
10:15					
10:30					
10:45					
11:00					
11:15					
11:30					
11:45					

Appendix

PM Schedule

	Monday	Tuesday	Wednesday	Thursday	Friday
DATE	DATE	DATE	DATE	DATE	DATE
12:00	12:00	12:00	12:00	12:00	12:00
12:15	12:15	12:15	12:15	12:15	12:15
12:30	12:30	12:30	12:30	12:30	12:30
12:45	12:45	12:45	12:45	12:45	12:45
1:00	1:00	1:00	1:00	1:00	1:00
1:15	1:15	1:15	1:15	1:15	1:15
1:30	1:30	1:30	1:30	1:30	1:30
1:45	1:45	1:45	1:45	1:45	1:45
2:00	2:00	2:00	2:00	2:00	2:00
2:15	2:15	2:15	2:15	2:15	2:15
2:30	2:30	2:30	2:30	2:30	2:30
2:45	2:45	2:45	2:45	2:45	2:45
3:00	3:00	3:00	3:00	3:00	3:00
3:15	3:15	3:15	3:15	3:15	3:15
3:30	3:30	3:30	3:30	3:30	3:30
3:45	3:45	3:45	3:45	3:45	3:45

Rigby Best Teachers Press

Small Reading Group Levels

Teacher _____ Grade _____ Date _____

PRE-EMERGENT
F&P: A

EMERGENT 1 F&P: B	**EMERGENT 2** F&P: C	**EMERGENT 3** F&P: D
EARLY 1 F&P: E	**EARLY 2** F&P: F	**EARLY 3** F&P: G, H
TRANSITIONAL 1 F&P: I, J	**TRANSITIONAL 2** F&P: K	**TRANSITIONAL 3** F&P: L, M
FLUENT 1 F&P: N, O	**FLUENT 2** F&P: P, Q, R	**FLUENT 3** F&P: S, T, U, V

PROFICIENT
F&P: W, X, Y, Z

Note: F&P = Fountas and Pinnell Levels

Appendix

Small Reading Group Notes

Lesson plans for the week of: _____ to _____. Group: _____

Monday	Tuesday	Wednesday	Thursday	Friday
Text:	Text:	Text:	Text:	Text:
Planned Teaching Points:	Planned Teaching Points:	Planned Teaching Points:	Planned Teaching Points:	Planned Teaching Points:
Notes:	Notes:	Notes:	Notes:	Notes:

Anecdotal notes on students:

Student:	Student:	Student:	Student:	Student:

148 Rigby Best Teachers Press

© Harcourt Achieve Inc. All rights reserved.

Name _____

I'm learning to…	I can…

Appendix

Emergent Reading Checklist

Name _____ Grade _____ Age _____

Knowledge of print behavior and strategies	Date/Comments
Enjoys listening to stories	
Uses reading-like behavior to approximate book language	
Uses meaning of the story to make predictions	
Chooses to read from various sources	
Notices and reads environmental print	
Can sit for a time and read a book	
Participates confidently in shared reading	
Retells stories and rhymes	
Likes to write	
Understands that writers use letter symbols to construct meaning	
Can show the front cover of book	
Understands that the print carries the message	
Uses pictures as clues to the story line	
Knows where to start reading the text	
Knows where to stop reading the text	
Knows which way to go, L–R, and return	
Knows which way to go, top to bottom	
Can point and match 1:1 as teacher reads	
Knows sounds and names of a few letters	
Can indicate and recognize few/some words	
Can indicate the space between the words	
Understands the difference between letters and words	
Can recognize some high-frequency words both in and out of context	
Can write some high-frequency words independently	

From *Rigby Literacy* © 2004 Rigby. Reprinted with permission.

Early Reading Checklist

Name _____ Grade _____ Date _____

	Date/Comments
Independent Reading	
Chooses to read independently	
Chooses to read nonfiction for independent reading	
Chooses to read narrative texts for independent reading	
Confidently shares feelings about texts	
Whole Class Reading	
Confidently participates in shared reading experiences	
Enjoys listening to books	
Shares experiences and background knowledge	
Reads in phrases or chunks	
Follows directions and procedures	
Responds to text to show understanding of comprehension strategies	
Responds to text to show understanding of content	
Small Group Reading	
Participates in small-group reading	
Engaged before, during, after reading	
Relies more on word cues than on picture cues	
Uses alphabetic knowledge to locate information	
Recognizes and reads an extended core of high-frequency words	
Uses decoding skills	
Rereads to check meaning	
Notices miscues and works at correcting them	
Uses comprehension strategies to construct deep meaning	
Confirms predictions using context	
Confirms predictions using graphophonic details	
Uses prior knowledge to help construct meaning	
Self-monitors by asking questions: Does it make sense? sound right? look right?	
Responses show understanding of text	

From *Rigby Literacy* © 2004 Rigby. Reprinted with permission.

Appendix

Fluent Reading Checklist

Name _____ Grade _____ Date _____

	Date/Comments
Independent Reading	
Enjoys reading independently	
Reads chapter books	
Chooses to read nonfiction for independent reading	
Chooses to read a variety of genres for independent reading	
Shares responses and texts with others	
Whole Class Reading	
Confidently participates in shared reading experiences	
Listens to all types of texts: chapter books, picture books, nonfiction selections	
Shares experiences and background knowledge	
Demonstrates understanding of the purpose for reading	
Shows confidence when reading unseen text	
Uses features of nonfiction texts to understand content	
Engaged before, during, and after reading	
Responds to text to show understanding of comprehension strategies	
Responds to text to show understanding of content	
Asks questions before, during, and after reading	
Follows directions and procedures	
Exhibits appropriate social behaviors	
Small Group Reading	
Confidently participates in small-group reading	
Demonstrates understanding of the purpose for reading	
Engaged before, during, and after reading	
Shows confidence when reading unseen text	
Uses comprehension strategies to construct deep meaning	
Monitors reading rate to ensure comprehension	
Responds to text to show understanding of comprehension strategies	
Responds to text to show understanding of content	

From *Rigby Literacy* © 2004 Rigby. Reprinted with permission.

Teaching Routines Checklist

	Routines	Date introduced	Dates revisited
Using materials			
Managing noise levels			
Getting help			
Getting students' attention			
Working inside the classroom (alone and with others)			
Working outside the classroom			

Appendix

Icons

Reading

Writing

Science

Social Studies

Math

Computer

Choice

Word Zone

Literature Circle

Appendix

Icons *(continued)*

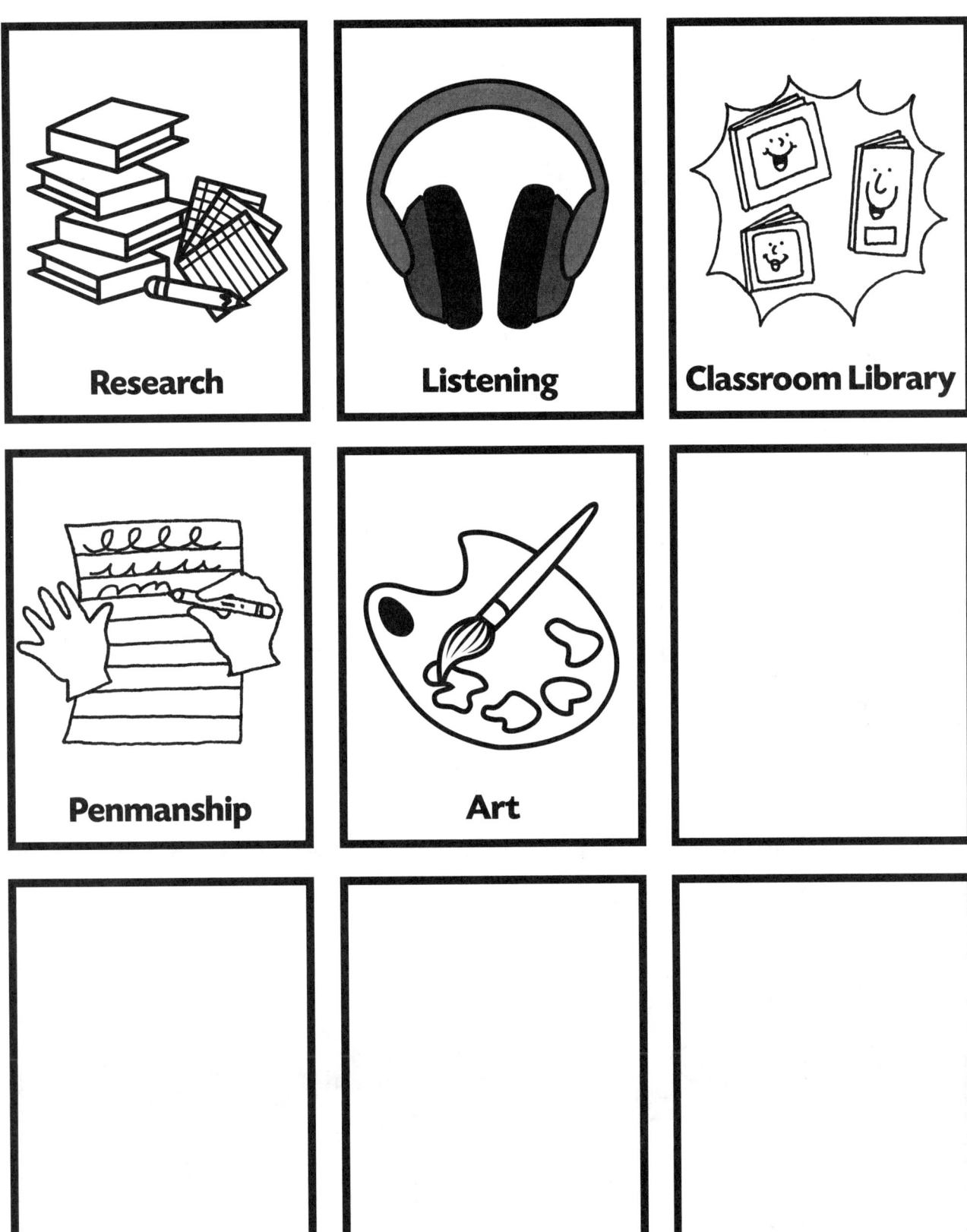

Appendix

Group Icons

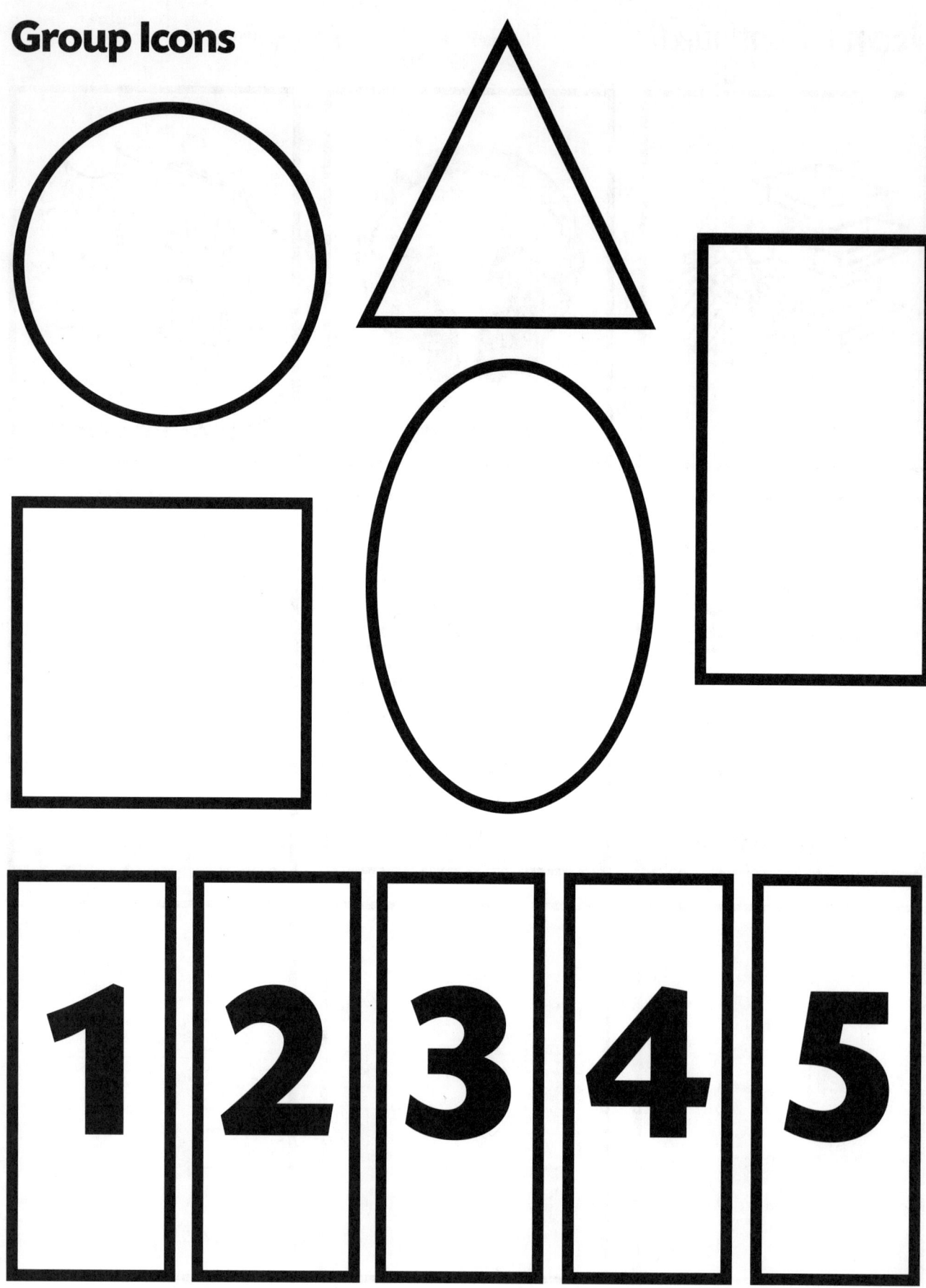

Contract

Name _____   Week of _____

Choices	Mon.	Tues.	Wed.	Thurs.	Fri.

Did you make good decisions this week? _____
Write about what you learned this week. _____
_____
_____

Parent Signature _____
Comments _____
_____

Adapted from *Rigby Literacy*. © 2000 Rigby. Reprinted with permission.

Appendix

Using Pictures To Prompt Writing

Note the opportunities for differentiating instruction by ability level or instructional focus. Be sure to introduce options over time, and precede each task with plenty of discussion and modeling.

Labels
Identify items in the picture, stretch out the words, and record the sounds.

Using Adjectives
Identify items in the picture, and label them using one or more describing words.

Snowballs
Identify an item in the picture and build a growing list, describing the object.

```
dog
small dog
small furry dog
small furry brown dog
```

Story Writing

1. Describe what is happening in the picture.
   The boy is walking his dog.

2. Add names and other details to make your story more interesting.
   John is walking his dog Spot. Spot likes to go for walks in the park.

3. Add dialogue to the story.
   "Come on, Spot!" yelled John. "Let's go for a walk..."

4. Write what happened before and/or after, as well as during the picture.
   The blizzard lasted for three days! Finally John's mother let him go outside. "Whoopee!" yelled John...

5. "This reminds me of ..." (Instead of writing about the picture, write the story it makes you think of from your own experiences.)
   "Brandy!" said my mom. "Brandy McMuffin of Hayden is what we'll call her."

Odds and Ends

1. Write lists related to the picture. (i.e., things you wear when it's cold, pets, pet names, etc.)

2. What kinds of things might you hear people saying here?

3. Write a letter to or from one of the people in the picture.

Rigby Best Teachers Press

Bibliography

Allington, Richard. 2001. *What really matters for struggling readers: Designing researched-based programs.* New York: Addison Wesley Longman.

Beatles. 1967. *I get by with a little help from my friends.* Capitol Records.

Bernstein, Lisa. August 20, 2004. Personal communication via telephone.

Bickart, Toni S., Jablon, Judy R., & Dodge, Trister, Diane. 1999. *Building the primary classroom: A complete guide to teaching and learning.* Washington, DC: Teaching Strategties.

Bruner, Jerome. 1960. *The process of education.* Cambridge, MA: Harvard University Press.

Caine, Renate Nummela, & Caine, Geoffrey. 1994. *Making connections: Teaching and the human brain.* Menlo Park, CA: Addison-Wesley.

Caine, Renate Nummela, & Caine, Geoffrey. 1997. *Education on the edge of possibility.* Alexandria, VA: Association for Supervision and Curriculum Development.

Calkins, Lucy. 1987. *In the middle.* Portsmouth, NH: Boynton/Cook Publishers.

Calkins, Lucy. 1999. *Re-imagining the reading/writing workshop.* Portsmouth, NH: Heinemann Workshops.

Calkins, Lucy, Montgomery, Kate, & Santman, Donna. 1998. *A teacher's guide to standardized reading tests: Knowledge is power.* Portsmouth, NH: Heinemann.

Cambourne, Brian. 1988. *The whole story.* Auckland, New Zealand: Ashton Scholastic.

Charles, C. M. 1998. *Building classroom discipline.* New York: Longman.

Clancy, Mary. August 28, 2004. Personal communication via electronic mail.

Clay, Marie. 1993. *An observation survey.* Portsmouth, NH: Heinemann.

Covey, Stephen R. 1989. *The seven habits of highly effective people.* New York, NY: Simon and Schuster.

Cunningham, Patricia M. 1995. *Phonics they use: Words for reading and writing.* New York: HarperCollins College Publishers.

Dangerous Minds. 1995. Produced by Don Simpson and Jerry Bruckheimer. Directed by John N. Smith. 99 minutes. Buena Vista Entertainment. Videocassette.

Danielson, Charlotte. 1996. *Enhancing professional practice: A framework for teaching.* Alexandria, VA: Association for Supervision and Curriculum Development.

Dorn, Linda J., French, Cathy, & Jones, Tammy. 1998. *Apprenticeship in literacy: Transitions across reading and writing.* York, ME: Stenhouse Publishers.

Education Department of South Australia. 1991. *Assessment of writing and reading inservice teacher education: Literacy asessment in practice: R-7 language arts.* Adelaide: Author.

Elting, Mary. 1980. *Q is for duck.* New York: Houghton Mifflin Company.

Everston, Carolyn M., Emmer, Edmond T., & Worsham, Murray E. 2003. *Classroom management for elementary teachers.* Boston, MA: Allyn and Bacon.

Fisher, Bobbi. 1991. *Joyful learning.* Portsmouth, NH: Heinemann.

Forester, Anne, & Reinhard, Margaret. 1994. *The teacher's way.* Winnipeg, Manitoba: Peguis Publishers.

Fountas, Irene C., & Pinnell, Gay Su. 1996. *Guided reading: Good first teaching for all children.* Portsmouth, NH: Heinemann.

Fountas, Irene C., & Pinnell, Gay Su. 2001. *Guiding readers and writers Grades 3-6: Teaching comprehension, genre, and content literacy.* Portsmouth, NH: Heinemann.

Glasser, William. 1993. *The quality school teacher.* New York: HarperPerennial.

Goodman, Amy. August 13, 2004. Personal communication via electronic mail.

Graves, Donald. 1994. *A fresh look at writing.* Portsmouth, NH: Heinemann.

Groeber, Joan. 2001. *Power of poetry.* Barrington, IL: Rigby.

Harste, Jerome C., Short, Kathy G., & Burke, Carolyn. 1988. *Creating classrooms for authors: The reading-writing connection.* Portsmouth, NH: Heinemann.

Hart, L. A. 1983. *Human brain, human learning.* New York: Longman.

Harvey, Stephanie, & Goudvis, Anne. 2000. *Strategies that work: Teaching comprehension to enhance understanding.* York, ME: Stenhouse Publishers.

Bibliography

Hill, Bonnie Campbell, Ruptic, Cynthia, & Norwick, Lisa. 1998. *Classroom based assessment.* Norwood, MA: Christopher-Gordon Publishers.

Hindley, Joanne. 1996. *In the company of children.* York, ME: Stenhouse Publishers.

Holdaway, Don. 1979. *The foundations of literacy.* Gosford, New South Wales: Ashton Scholastic.

Jensen, Eric. 1995. *Brain-based learning.* San Diego, CA: The Brain Store Publishing.

Jensen, Eric. 1998. *Teaching with the brain in mind.* Alexandria, VA: Association for Supervision and Curriculum Development.

Kagan, Spencer. 1992. *Cooperative learning.* San Clemente, CA: Kagan.

Keene, Ellin Oliver, & Zimmermann, Susan. 1997. *Mosaic of thought.* Portsmouth, NH: Heinemann.

Kohn, Alfie. 1993. *Punished by rewards: The trouble with gold stars, incentive plans, A's, praise, and other bribes.* New York: Houghton Mifflin Company.

Kohn, Alfie. 1998. *What to look for in a classroom... and other essays.* San Francisco, CA: Jossey-Bass.

Kovalik, Susan J., & Olsen, Karen D. 2002 *Exceeding expectations: A user's guide to implementing brain research in the classroom.* Covington, WA: Susan Kovalik and Associates.

McDonald, Beth. August 17, 2004. Personal communication via electronic mail.

Mooney, Margaret. 1990. *Reading to, with, and by children.* Katonah, NY: Richard C. Owen Publishers.

Nations, Susan, & Alonso, Mellissa. 2001. *Primary literacy centers: Making reading and writing stick!* Gainesville, FL: Maupin House Publishing.

Ohlihausen, Marliyn M., & Jepsin, Mary. 1992. Lessons from Goldilocks: "Somebody's been choosing my books but I can make my own choices now! *The New Advocate,* 5, 36.

Pearson, P.D., & Gallagher, M.C. 1983. The instruction of reading comprehension. *Contemporary Educational Psychology,* 8, 317–344.

Platt, Robyn. 1996. *ELIC Facilitator Training,* Rigby Education: Barrington, IL.

Routman, Regie. 2000. *Conversations.* Portsmouth, NH: Heinemann.

Routman, Regie. 2003. *Reading essentials.* Portsmouth, NH: Heinemann.

Servis, Joan. 1999. *Celebrating the fourth.* Portsmouth, NH: Heinemann.

Seuss, Dr. 1963. *Dr. Seuss' abc.* New York: Random House.

Silverstein, Shel. 1964. *The giving tree.* New York: HarperCollins Publishers.

Silverstein, Shel. 1974. *Where the sidewalk ends.* New York: HarperCollins Children's Books.

Shannon, George. 1996. *Tomorrow's alphabet.* New York: Scholastic.

Smith, Frank. 1985. *Reading without nonsense.* New York: Teachers College Press.

Smith, Frank. 1986. *Insult to intelligence.* Portsmouth, NH: Heinemann.

Sylwester, Robert. 1998. *The downshifting dilemma: A commentary and proposal.* Seattle, WA: New Horizons for Learning.

Taberski, Sharon. 2000. *On solid ground.* Portsmouth, NH: Heinemann.

Taberski, Sharon. 1996. *A close-up look at teaching reading: Focusing on children and our goals.* 80 minutes. Portsmouth, NH: Heinemann.

Tierney, R. J., Readence, J. E., & Dishner, E. K. 1990. *Reading strategies and practices: A compendium* (3rd ed.). Boston: Allyn & Bacon.

Van Allsburg, Chris. 1987. *The z was zapped.* New York: Houghton Mifflin Company.

Veatch, Jeanette. 1959. *Individualizing your reading program.* New York: Putnam.

Veatch, Jeanette. 1997. In-district literacy in-service CUSD 220. Barrington, IL.

Vygotsky, Fyodor. 1962. *Thought and language.* Cambridge, MA: MIT Press and Wiley.

Wagstaff, Janiel M. 1999. *Teaching reading and writing with word walls: Easy lessons and fresh ideas for creating interactive word walls that build literacy skills.* New York: Scholastic.

Webb, Beth. October 15, 1999. Conversation with author.

Wong, Harry. 1998. *The first days of school.* Mountain View, CA: Harry K. Wong Publications.